John Foote Norton

The record of Athol, Massachusetts, in suppressing the great rebellion

John Foote Norton

The record of Athol, Massachusetts, in suppressing the great rebellion

ISBN/EAN: 9783337208240

Printed in Europe, USA, Canada, Australia, Japan

Cover: Foto ©ninafisch / pixelio.de

More available books at **www.hansebooks.com**

THE

RECORD OF ATHOL,

MASSACHUSETTS,

In Suppressing the Great Rebellion.

PREPARED FOR PUBLICATION
BY A COMMITTEE OF THE TOWN.

BOSTON:
PRINTED BY GEO. C. RAND & AVERY,
1866.

To the

Athol Soldiers

WHO HASTENED TO THE RESCUE WHEN

TREASON RAISED ITS HAND TO DRAW THE LIFE-BLOOD OF OUR

BELOVED COUNTRY;

To the

Families and Kindred

OF THESE HEROIC MEN,

WHO CHEERED THEM ON IN THIS MIGHTY STRUGGLE TILL

THE NATION WAS SAVED; AND ESPECIALLY

To the

Memory of the Dead

WHO FELL IN THIS CONFLICT, AND SEALED THEIR

ATTACHMENT TO LIBERTY AND RIGHT WITH THEIR BLOOD,

THIS VOLUME IS

Respectfully Dedicated.

INTRODUCTION.

In presenting this Volume to the people of Athol and to her sons and daughters who residing elsewhere still cherish a deep interest in all that appertains to her honor the undersigned would make the following Statements respecting the Origin of the work, the object they have kept steadily in view while preparing it, the sources of information to which they have had access and the assistance they have received in their difficult and responsible undertaking.

In the Warrant for the Town Meeting of Athol for April 7. 1862, Article 4th was as follows.

"To see if the Town will choose a Committee to collect and preserve facts and incidents which may have a historic interest to the people of the Town as showing the part they have taken in aiding to suppress the Great Rebellion."

At the Town Meeting held under this War-

rant it was "Voted to choose a Committee of
three to collect and preserve such facts as they
may think best; and said Committee will work
free of charge to the Town. Chose Rev. John
F. Norton John M. Twichell and Dr. A. G. Williams; and then voted to add one and chose Dr.
James P. Lynde."

This Committee was organized by the appointment of Rev. John F. Norton, Chairman, and
Dr. J. P. Lynde Secretary.

Dr. A. G. Williams having accepted a commission as a Surgeon in the Army, at a Town
Meeting March 2. 1863 Mr. Charles W. Bannon
was added to the Committee at the request of
the other members. He had previously rendered much assistance in collecting and arranging many of the facts that relate to the early
history of recruiting in Athol.

At the Town Meeting Nov. 7. 1865, on motion of Nathaniel Richardson Esqr it was "Voted
that the Town authorize its Committee in charge
to publish by subscription the Record entitled
'Athol in Suppressing the Great Rebellion' with
such changes as said Committee may deem desirable."

"Voted that the Selectmen be authorized to
subscribe in the name of the Town for Fifty
Copies of the Record, provided it can be fur-

nished at a price not exceeding two dollars per copy."

Immediately after its appointment the Committee entered upon its work by collecting the names of all the soldiers who had enlisted from Athol and recording the same with the Regiments and Companies with which they were connected. A record was also made of all that the Town had done during the year 1861 to encourage enlistments and also of the various movements on the part of our citizens during the same period to give to our imperilled Union an efficient army. Since March 1862 the Record has been kept as events have transpired; and in transcribing all this for the press, such additional explanations have been made as a full and easy understanding of the whole matter seemed to require.

It has been our object in preparing this Volume to collect and place upon record in an intelligible form such facts, and such only as may be of permanent value. The history of such events as we have here undertaken to preserve soon becomes confused amid the stirring life of our American people; and it has been our aim to rescue this, so far as the Town of Athol is concerned, from being either corrupted by rumors of doubtful authority or lost in the ordinary course of human forgetfulness. Hardly a City

1*

or Town in our land has in its possession a particular and reliable history of what it did to maintain the cause of the American Revolution, of the sacrifices it made, of the heroes that it furnished, of the martyrs to liberty that went out from it never to return. What a value should we now attach to such a Record! With what an interest should we turn over its almost sacred leaves! Precisely such a history of the part Athol has taken in suppressing the Great Rebellion we have endeavored to furnish for those who shall come after us. It has been our aim to select the most important facts relative . to our experience in this eventful struggle and to transmit them, in a legible form, to our children and children's children, that if they shall not know precisely what American Liberty cost at the first, they may have at least some correct impressions respecting the sacrifices required for its preservation. That our judgment has never been in fault in selecting materials for this Volume, we have not the presumption to suppose. Others would have omitted perhaps some things that we have inserted, and recorded upon these pages matters that we have not regarded as particularly important; all that we can say is that we have endeavored to preserve to the fullest extent possible, such facts and incidents

as we have deemed to be of the greatest permanent value.

The general plan of the work, we have reason
to suppose is all that can be desired. The Index
of Soldiers' Names and the General Index will
make the reference to any particular event or
to the personal history of any Athol man who
served in the Army or Navy, easy.

The Historical Narrative will contain a faithful record of what the Town in its corporate
capacity has done in furnishing men and means
to maintain the struggle with treason, and with
this not a little valuable information respecting
the sacrifices of particular families and individuals upon the altar of our Common Country.

The Tables in which the men that we have
furnished appear in their Regiments, Companies
&c. present to the eye, at once, a multitude of
interesting facts with which but few now can be
supposed to be familiar and which those who
shall come after us will deem invaluable.

The pages upon which we have recorded the
personal experience of Athol men in the war,
and which have cost the Committee a vast
amount of labor, will be interesting to the great
mass of this community at any time; but plainly
they will be deemed more and more important
as the actors in these scenes shall give place to
other generations and our posterity shall ask

how their fathers demeaned themselves in the Great Conflict. This part of our Record we are confident presents but little of which to be ashamed.

With regard to the sources of information to which we have had access in preparing this Volume we would say that in general they have been of the highest authority. In all possible cases official records have been consulted and carefully followed. The votes of the Town have been copied from the Town Records, and the proceedings of the Selectmen in all the matters appertaining to the aid rendered Soldiers' families and to the business of enlistments and paying bounties, we have copied from their official papers. We have been also greatly aided by the Muster Rolls and Memorials of Companies, while in nearly every case the history of our men in the war has been obtained through personal interviews or correspondence. In bringing together and arranging such a mass of materials mistakes have doubtless occurred, but we have constantly aimed to have every part of the Volume worthy of confidence.

For important aid rendered us in keeping this Record and now giving it to the public, our thanks are due to the Gentlemen who have constituted the Board of Selectmen of Athol since the commencement of the Great Rebellion.

Particularly have we received the most valuable assistance from Calvin Kelton Esqr who has been Chairman of this Board during the whole period covered by this history, with the exception of a single year. Mr Kelton's excellent business habits which have rendered successful the administration of our Town affairs during these years of unexampled expenditure, have made a part of our labors in preparing this work comparatively easy, while in many cases of doubt we have freely availed ourselves of his valuable assistance. The work of bringing together and arranging in proper form the several amounts of money contributed to pay Citizen's Bounties under the different calls for troops during the year 1864 has been willingly and successfully done at the suggestion of the Committee by Mr. Henry Martyn Humphrey and Mr. Lucian Lord. The value of the aid rendered us by these Young Gentlemen will appear by consulting the record commencing upon page 109. of this Volume.

In procuring Subscribers for this Book we have been greatly assisted by Sergeant Enoch T. Lewis, Corporal Levi B. Fay, Jonathan Drury Esqr and by Messrs Isaac King, J. B. Wheeler, Ira Y. Kendall, Benjamin M. Twichell Jr., Cyrus Stockwell and Isaiah S. Merrill of Athol and Mr Dexter Aldrich of Boston.

The other Members of the Committee deem it

due to their Chairman Rev. John F. Norton, to
state that the labor of collecting most of the
materials for this Volume, of making all the entries in the Book of Records and of preparing
the whole for the press has been performed by
him.

JOHN F. NORTON ⎫
JOHN M. TWICHELL ⎪
ALFRED G. WILLIAMS ⎬ *Committee.*
JAMES P. LYNDE ⎪
CHARLES W. BANNON ⎭

ATHOL, MASS., Jan. 1866.

NOTE. The Chairman of the Committee is alone responsible
for any peculiarities in the typography of this Volume.

SOLDIERS' INDEX.

———◆◇◆———

14 INDEX.

2*

GENERAL INDEX.

HISTORICAL NARRATIVE.

THE people of Athol, Mass., in common with all their loyal countrymen, were filled with amazement and the most gloomy apprehensions, by the bombardment of Fort Sumter, a fortress of the United States, in the harbor of Charleston, S.C. The attack upon this fort, which was the opening scene of the Great Rebellion, was made April 12, 1861 ; and the little garrison, under the heroic Col. (afterwards Gen.) Robert Anderson, surrendered to the rebel hosts that assailed it, after a bold resistance for the space of about thirty-six hours.

Washington was at once menaced by an army of rebels that poured into Virginia. But a few days elapsed before Massachusetts men were shot in the streets of Baltimore, while on their way to rescue the National Capital. The whole South was in commotion; and every hour the rebel cause gained strength, till it assumed the most frightful proportions.

The news of these events aroused all the patriotism of the North ; and the people of Athol determined to do their part for the support of our government against the mighty combination that threatened to destroy it. From all parts of the town men, women and children came together to raise and honor the glorious flag of our Union, and to determine upon the course of action which the crisis demanded. Processions were formed, and the gatherings in different parts of the town were large and enthusiastic.

At a public meeting in the Town Hall, on the evening of April 19, 1861, a number of young men came forward, and offered themselves for the formation of a military company. Forty or more were ready to leave at once to defend the Nation's Capital. The process of drilling was commenced ; but, after more mature deliberation, the formation of a military company was postponed for a season. It should be remarked, however, that most of the individuals who offered themselves as soldiers from Athol at that early period, subsequently enlisted and were mustered into the service of the United States, in different companies and regiments of the Massachusetts Volunteers.

April 30, 1861. — At a town-meeting legally called, Calvin Kelton Esq., being moderator, upon the recommendation of a committee, consisting of C. C. Bassett Esq., Hon. Charles Field, Nathaniel Richardson Esq., L. W. Hapgood Esq. and Mr. John Kendall, it was voted, "that five thousand dollars be appropriated" for the purpose of encouraging men to volunteer for military service; and "that ten dollars per month be given to each unmarried volunteer, and twenty dollars to each married volunteer, in addition to the pay insured them by the laws of the United States. And, "if more be necessary to support the families of the married volunteers, the committee is to make up the deficiency. The volunteers above referred to are those from Athol, called the Athol Company of Volunteers."

The meeting at which the votes above mentioned were taken was large; and the voters of Athol were nearly unanimous in making the appropriation.

If any discover a lack of definiteness and legal precision in this early action of the town to encourage enlistments in the army, it should be remembered that all was new and strange, and that the excitement of the people under which this meeting was held was intense. Whatever else was wanting at that early day, the people of Athol did not lack the spirit of self-denial and genuine patriotism.

Enlistments soon commenced. The first to leave their homes for the camp and the years of

3

hard service before them were sixteen young men, who joined the Second Regiment of Massachusetts Volunteers, under Col. George H. Gordon. This regiment was in camp at West Roxbury, from May to July 8, 1861, when it received marching orders, and left for the Upper Potomac.

The first man from Athol who signed the enlistment-roll, and was mustered into the United States service, was Leander W. Phelps, one of the sixteen above named. The names of these young men are here given as follows: Leander W. Phelps, David E. Billings, J. B. Billings, Delevan Richardson, Hubbard V. Smith, Edward L. Townsend, Charles H. Hill, Charles S. Green, Columbus Fox, William L. Clutterbuck, Horace Hunt, William Nute, Frederic Cummings, John D. Emerson, Thomas Johnson and Aurin B. French. The services of these young men, who have the honor of having their names at the head of the long list of Athol soldiers, will be detailed at considerable length in other parts of this record.

The Tenth Regiment went to the seat of war a few days later than the Second, and in this were two young men from Athol; viz., John F. Merrill and James L. Merrill. These soldiers, who did good service, belonged to Company H, recruited in Shelburne.

Before any money was actually used under

the vote of the town at the meeting, April 30, 1861, another meeting of the legally qualified voters of Athol was called " To see if the town will raise and appropriate money for the support of the families of those residents who have enlisted, or may enlist, and go into the service of the United States Government, according to the provisions of a recent statute of the Commonwealth." This meeting was holden July 10, 1861, and was not largely attended by the voters of Athol.   Its action was, however, very important, as will be seen by the votes that were passed as follows : —

" *Voted*, That two dollars per week shall be paid out of the treasury of the town to the wife or parent of any inhabitant of the town, who has enlisted or may enlist in the service of the United States Government during the present war, provided such wife or parent was or is dependent upon such inhabitant for support.

" *Voted*, That one dollar per week shall be paid out of the treasury of the town to each child, under sixteen years of age, of any inhabitant of the town, who has enlisted or may enlist in the service of the United States Government during the present war, who is dependent upon said parent for support.

" *Voted*, In case of sickness of any inhabitant entitled to benefit according to the previous sections, the expenses of medical attendance shall be paid out of the treasury of the town.

"*Voted*, That the amount due the above inhabitants shall be paid monthly, or oftener, if needed."

Under the above-mentioned action of the town, enlistments soon began to be numerous, the men connecting themselves with the various regiments that were assembling in different parts of the Commonwealth. Twenty-three at this time joined the Twenty-first Regiment, which was recruited at Camp Lincoln, Worcester. This regiment, which did good service for three years, left for the seat of war, Aug. 22, 1861, and took charge of the railroad leading from Annapolis, Md., to Baltimore and Washington. Most of the twenty-three men who went with it from Athol were connected with Company A, which was recruited in Templeton, and commanded by Capt., and afterwards Major and Lieut.-Col. George P. Hawkes. This company was called "The Adams Guards." The names of these men, and a brief account of their services and sufferings, will be found in their proper place in this record.

Soon after the Twenty-first Regiment left for Annapolis, viz. in September, 1861, another and successful effort was made to recruit a company in Athol and vicinity, to be commanded by Adin

W. Caswell. This gentleman, who had already had some experience in military matters, undertook this work; and, in the short space of ten days, the requisite number of men was obtained. The examination of these recruits was made by Dr. A. G. Williams of Athol, who was commissioned for this purpose. On the 4th of October, 1861, which was the day of the Annual Cattleshow and Fair, a dinner was given to this company on the Common at Athol; and the men were addressed from the balcony of the Summit House. Dr. James P. Lynde presided and addressed the soldiers and the immense audience which assembled. A sword, sash, &c., were presented to Capt. Caswell, Hon. Charles Field making the address of presentation. Capt. Caswell responded, and addresses were afterwards made by Hiram Woodward Esq. of Orange; James Brooks Esq. of Petersham; J. H. Goddard Esq., Editor of "The Barre Gazette;" Rev. I. S. Lincoln, of Warwick; Rev. A. Harding, of New Salem; and Calvin Kelton Esq., Chairman of the Board of Selectmen; Rev. Ira Bailey and Rev. John F. Norton, of Athol. A patriotic poem, which he had prepared for the occasion, was recited by Rev. D. J. Mandell, also of Athol. Bouquets of flowers were presented to all the soldiers composing the company, by young ladies who volunteered for this service; while patriotic

3*

songs, in which a multitude of voices joined, enlivened the occasion. The exercises at the Summit House were closed with prayer by Rev. J. F. Norton; and almost the entire assembly went with the company to the depot, where the soldiers took the cars for the encampment at Springfield. The Athol Cornet Band was present during the day, and added to its interest; while the Athol High School Guard, under the command of the master of said school, Mr. Andrew J. Lathrop, with fifty mounted men of Athol, and nearly the same number from Royalston, did escort duty. The company left with the cheers and benedictions of the assembled multitude.

At Springfield, these soldiers were mustered into the service of the United States, and constituted Company B of the Twenty-seventh Regiment, Massachusetts Volunteers.

The chief officers of this regiment, which left Camp Reed, Springfield, for Annapolis, Md., Nov. 2, 1861, were as follows:—

Horace C. Lee, Springfield, Colonel; Luke Lyman, Northampton, Lieutenant-Colonel; William M. Brown, Major; George W. Bartlett, Greenfield, Adjutant; George A. Otis, Springfield, Surgeon; Samuel Camp, Great Barrington, Assistant-Surgeon; Rev. Miles Sanford, Adams, Chaplain.

The regiment was known as the Second Western Regiment of Massachusetts Volunteers. The commissioned officers of Company B were as follows: —

Adin W. Caswell, Athol, Captain; Parker W. McManus, Davenport, Ia., First Lieutenant; Lovell H. Horton, Athol, Second Lieutenant.

At a later period, while the regiment was at Annapolis, a dinner was given to Company B by its friends in Athol and vicinity, the part from Athol being despatched by express in thirteen large packages.

In the band of music attached to the Twenty-seventh Regiment were six young gentlemen from Athol; viz., Thomas Kenney, Joseph F. Fay, William Richardson, Henry T. Morse, Leander B. Morse, and George R. Hanson. The four last mentioned were, at a later period, attached to other regiments in the same department of service. The names of all the men belonging to Company B will be given in the history of the services of that regiment.

Later in the year 1861, arrangements were made to recruit another company in Athol and vicinity for the Butler Expedition; but, through a misunderstanding between the State Executive and Major-Gen. Butler, the proposed regiment was not raised, and the matter was dropped while the prospects for the recruiting of the company were good. A number of men from Athol, however, enlisted for the Thirtieth and

Thirty-first Regiments, that went to Ship Island in the Gulf of Mexico, and afterwards to New Orleans under Gen. Butler.

During the autumn of 1861, a number of young men from Athol enlisted for the First Battalion of Infantry, which was stationed at Fort Warren, Boston Harbor. This battalion, which was raised with special reference to garrison duty at Fort Warren, and for guarding the political and war prisoners confined there, in 1862 became the Thirty-second Regiment of Massachusetts Volunteers, and did good service till the close of the war.

In the warrant for the town-meeting in Athol Nov. 5, 1861, the fourth article was as follows:—

" To see if the town will rescind any or all votes passed at a town-meeting held on the tenth day of July, 1861, whereby they voted to pay a certain amount to the families of volunteers; and also for medical expenses of the same in case of sickness."

At the meeting held under this warrant it was "*Voted*, 1. That as to all inhabitants who may hereafter, as members of the volunteer militia of this State, be mustered into or enlisted in the service of the United States, there shall be raised, and, under the direction of the selectmen, paid for the aid of the wife, parent, or children under sixteen years of age, who are dependent upon such soldier for support, a sum not exceeding one dollar per week; provided the whole sum paid for all those persons so dependent upon such inhabitant shall not exceed twelve dollars per month.

"*Voted*, 2. So far as it relates to those already enlisted and now in the service of the United States, the medical attendance of the families shall be under the direction, and paid for at the discretion, of the selectmen.

"*Voted*, 3. That nothing be paid to the families of any volunteers, who were not inhabitants of the town for one month at least before enlisting into the service of the United States; and this shall apply to all past as well as future enlistments.

"*Voted*, 4. That all votes passed on the tenth day of July, 1861, so far as the same are inconsistent with the above votes, are repealed."

To understand the action of the town in passing the votes above recorded at the meeting, Nov. 5, 1861, it should be remembered that the State had assumed the payment of the aid to soldiers' families, but not to exceed twelve dollars per month to any family, however large it might be. Of course, the town of Athol was bound to pay all that had been promised to the soldiers who had been mustered into the United States service before the above-mentioned meeting of Nov. 5; but the object aimed at was to reduce the amount of aid offered, in case of future enlistments, to the sum promised by the State; viz., to twelve dollars per month.

To understand the third vote passed at the meeting of Nov. 5, it should be mentioned, that as the town of Athol was paying, under the votes of July 10, to soldiers with large families, more than was offered by the adjoining towns, an inducement was offered to soldiers already in the service, from other places, who had large families, to remove to Athol for the purpose of securing a larger sum of weekly or monthly aid. The Vote No. 3, above recorded, was designed to prevent any movement of this kind.

But as there was still some doubt in regard to the bearing of the votes passed at the town-meeting, Nov. 5, 1861, upon individual cases, another town-meeting was called for Dec. 6, 1861; and, at this meeting, it was

"*Voted*, 1. That there shall be paid out of the treasury of the town, under the direction of the selectmen, such sums of money as the selectmen shall deem necessary, not exceeding two dollars per week, for the aid of the wife or parent, and one dollar per week for the aid of each child under sixteen years of age, of any one of the inhabitants of said town, who, as members of the volunteer militia of this State, may have been mustered into the service of the United States between the fifteenth day of May, 1861, and the fifth day of November, 1861; provided such wife, parent, or child was dependent on such inhabitant for support.

"*Voted*, 2. That all votes passed on the tenth day of July last, inconsistent with the above vote, are hereby rescinded.

The first vote above recorded, while it affirmed the action of the town in the first vote of the meeting of July 10, so far as this related to the families of soldiers enlisting before Nov. 5, 1861, was chiefly important, because, conforming to the statute, it left the business of paying the money voted by the town to soldiers' families in the hands of the selectmen. Care and discretion were requisite in conducting this matter properly, and it was wisely required that this duty should devolve upon the selectmen.

For the year 1861, the Athol board of selectmen consisted of Calvin Kelton, Esq., chairman, A. L. Cheney, and John Kendall.

During the year 1861, or the first year of the war, twenty-eight individuals or families received money from the town under the several votes which had been passed for the aid of such as might be dependent upon Athol soldiers for support. The names of the soldiers, with the amounts received by their respective families, and the part of the same refunded to the town by the State, are here given as follows : —

	To aid,	Whole Amounts.	Refunded by the State.
Lewis P. Atwood,	Wife,	$18.00	9.00
J. B. Billings,	Mother,	64.00	32.00
John S. Briggs,	Wife & Children,	76.28	34.80
Eli Bodet,	Wife & Children,	14.80	14.80
Francis B. Brock,	Father,	12.14	12.14
W. L. Clutterbuck,	Wife & Child,	54.00	36.00
J. B. Cummings,	Wife & Child,	59.14	39.57
John M. Casavant,	Wife & Children,	13.60	13.60
Joseph H. Collins,	Wife,	39.14	19.57
Patrick Dempsey,	Wife & Children,	85.00	79.60
Aurin B. French,	Wife & Child,	96.00	64.43
Patrick W. Fox,	Mother,	39.14	19.57
Gardner Howe,	Wife & Children,	14.40	14.40
George W. Meacham,	Wife & Children,	102.84	35.20
George Morse,	Wife,	25.71	12.85
John O. Morey,	Wife & Children,	96.00	32.80
Norris B. Meacham,	Wife,	24.28	12.14
Edmund Moore,	Mother,	25.14	12.57
George W. Nelson,	Wife & Child,	9.72	9.72
James C. Parker,	Wife & Children,	105.00	57.20
Asa Phillips,	Wife,	10.00	00.00
William Richardson,	Wife & Child,	35.53	25.81
N. F. Ripley,	Child,	19.57	9.71
James H. Richardson,	Wife & Children,	50.86	26.06
Horace K. Weaver,	Wife & Child,	10.56	10.56
Morgan Young,	Wife,	38.57	19.28
Samuel A. Hill,	Wife,	37.43	18.71
William H. Johnson,	Mother,	37.43	18.71

The amount paid to the families of volunteers by the town of Athol, during the year 1861, was therefore $1,214.28, of which there was reimbursed by the State $690.70.

During the year 1861, the President of the United States issued three calls for troops to suppress the Rebellion. The first, April 16, 1861, was for seventy-five thousand men, for three months' service: the second, May 2, 1861, was for six regiments from Massachusetts, to serve for three years or for the war.

The third call, bearing date June 17, 1861, was for ten regiments, to serve for three years, or the war. The quotas for the several cities and towns in Massachusetts were not assigned under these calls; but it is believed that the number of men due from Athol was furnished.

At the close of the year 1861, Athol had in the service ninety-eight men enlisted for three years, or for the war, viz. two commissioned officers, Capt A. W. Caswell and second Lieut. L. H. Horton of Company B Twenty-seventh Regiment and ninety-six privates. Two of these, John Humphrey and Elijah W. Lincoln, were in the navy, while seven men had joined the regular army and were assigned to the eleventh United States Infantry.

The year 1861 closed with the rebels unsubdued and the Rebellion strong and defiant. Meanwhile, Major-Gen. McClellan had brought together a large army in the vicinity of Washington, which was constantly gaining in discipline and efficiency and Major-Gen. Burnside was collecting troops at Annapolis to fall in due time upon the coast of North Carolina.

1862.

At the opening of the year 1862, Athol having furnished between sixty and seventy men for the Burnside Expedition, which was about leaving Annapolis for some point upon the Southern coast, all eyes were turned toward that quarter with the deepest interest. The Twenty-first Regiment, in which Athol had twenty-three men, went on board the steamer " Northerner," Jan. 6. The Twenty-fifth Regiment, in which Athol had four men embarked at Annapolis, Jan. 7; while the Twenty-seventh Regiment, in which we had forty-one enlisted men, embarked Jan. 6. Jan. 11, 1862, all had arrived at Hampton Roads; and all sailed for the South under sealed orders, Jan. 12. A terrible storm was encountered on the passage, in which the transports were separated from one another and in imminent danger of shipwreck; while the men on board suffered greatly. Hatteras Inlet on the coast of North Carolina having been at length gained and the bar there having been finally crossed, the battle of Roanoke Island was fought and won on the 8th of February, 1862. In this, the men from Athol who were able to

leave the transports were engaged, and exposed
to a severe fire from the enemy. A cold drench-
ing rain fell after they had reached the shore,
while their course in marching to the attack lay
through almost impenetrable thickets and miry
swamps. Standing in the water, sometimes up
to their knees and even higher, while fighting
the enemy, some of our soldiers contracted colds
from which they never recovered, as will be seen
by turning to their personal history as contained
in this record. William Hill Company B Twenty-
seventh Regiment, was the first man killed in action from Athol, and he fell at the capture of
Roanoke Island. Patrick Leonard of Company
A Twenty-first Regiment, was also mortally
wounded in the same conflict. Capt. Caswell
being sick and on board a transport, Company B
of the Twenty-seventh Regiment was led in this
its first engagement with the rebels by first Lieutenant, Parker McMannus.

March 11, 1862, the regiments composing the
Burnside Expedition embarked from Roanoke
Island and on the 13th landed in the vicinity of
Newbern. On the 14th they engaged the enemy and captured that city after a bloody battle.
Of Company A Twenty-first Regiment, two men,
viz. James C. Parker and William H. Johnson,
both of Athol, were killed in that engagement,
while a number of others were severely wounded.

Company B of the Twenty-seventh Regiment was bravely led at Newbern by Capt. Caswell. All of the soldiers from Athol were in the thickest of the fight on that occasion, and did their duty manfully. On Thursday, March 20, the reports of the sufferings and loss, as well as victory of our men in North Carolina having reached Athol, a meeting of the citizens was held on the evening of that day. Rev. John F. Norton presided, and Mr. C. W. Bannon was chosen secretary. After various proposals, Laban Morse Esq. was appointed the agent of the people of Athol, to repair at once to Newbern and to aid, in every possible way, our sick and wounded soldiers. Mr. Morse left the next morning, March 21; two hundred and twenty-seven dollars having been contributed in a few hours to meet his expenses and to enable him most effectually to carry out the object of his mission. He arrived at Newbern, March 25, and was most joyfully greeted by our soldiers. Of money, there was scarcely any in the regiments, and the aid that Mr. Morse carried to them was timely. Every delicacy that he could procure for the sick and wounded was obtained, and the suffering soldiers from other towns were cared for equally with our own. Sleeping, rolled in his blanket, upon the floor in the hospital, that he might be ready for any service, Mr. Morse devoted all his energies to the welfare of the soldiers; and the many whom he was permitted to relieve and comfort will ever hold his name in grateful remembrance. After an absence of a little more than five weeks, he returned with a number of sick and wounded soldiers, and at a public meeting called to hear his report, May 5, 1862, a vote of thanks to him for his faithful and laborious service was unanimously passed. Money for the relief of the suffering under his command was left by Mr. Morse with Capt. Caswell, and from the funds which remained unexpended by him at the time of his return, assistance was, at a later period, rendered to our sick and exposed soldiers in various companies.

During the absence of Mr. Morse and at his suggestion, boxes of valuable hospital-stores were sent by the friends of the soldiers in Athol to our men in North Carolina, consigned to Dr. Otis, Surgeon of the Twenty-seventh Regiment.

It should be mentioned in this connection, that Mr. Morse declined any renumeration for his time and service as our agent in North Carolina.

Early in the year 1862, the work of suppressing the Rebellion was most vigorously prosecuted at the West; and, in April of that year, New Orleans was captured from the rebels, and

4*

the mouth of the Mississippi opened. Athol had a number of men in the army of Major-Gen. Butler, that was engaged in this important work.

May 28, 1862, another call was made by the President of the United States upon the Governor of this Commonwealth for additional troops, — three regiments of infantry to serve for three years, or till the end of the war, and one company of light artillery to serve for six months were asked for. Measures were at once adopted to furnish these, though recruiting at this time in Athol was not rapid.

July 4, 1862, the President issued an order for three hundred thousand volunteers to serve for three years, or until the end of the war, and with these, new regiments were to be formed and the ranks of such as were already in service were to be filled. The proportion assigned to Massachusetts was fifteen thousand men. The assessors' returns of the men liable to do military duty in the Commonwealth were used as the best basis that could then be obtained for deciding upon the number of men which each city and town ought to furnish. Under this call, the number assigned to Athol was forty-eight; and Aug. 2, 1862, a town-meeting was held to encourage enlistments.

At this meeting, the following preamble was

adopted, and the vote under it unanimously passed.

" *Whereas,* On the 4th day of July last, the President of the United States issued his Proclamation calling for three hundred thousand volunteers to be enlisted for three years; and

" *Whereas* the proportion or quota of such volunteers to be furnished by the town of Athol, in case of a draft, has been officially stated to be forty-eight: therefore

" *Voted,* That the selectmen of Athol be authorized, in behalf of the town, to pay a bounty of one hundred dollars to every inhabitant of the town who shall have enlisted since July 7, 1862, or shall hereafter, on or before the 16th day of August, 1862, enlist into said service, until the number equal to said quota shall be fully made up. Such payment shall be made as each of said volunteers shall be mustered into the service by the proper United States authority, and in the order that their names shall be returned, as so mustered, to the selectmen by any recruiting officer; provided however, that no bounty shall be paid by this town to any one who has received, or who is entitled to receive, a bounty from any other town or city."

Provision was made at the same meeting for raising the money that might be needed to pay bounties under the above vote of the town; and, in the course of a few days, forty-one men enlisted from Athol, received the promised bounty of one hundred dollars each, and were assigned to the different regiments of Massachusetts volunteers already in service, or helped to fill new regiments.   Twelve of these joined Company B of the Twenty-seventh Regiment; and the same number became connected with the various companies of the Thirty-sixth Regiment, which was recruited in Worcester County, and left Worcester for Washington, Sept. 2, 1862.   This regiment became a part of Gen. Burnside's army, which was then in camp near Sharpsburg, Md.

As this seems the proper place for inserting it, we here give the history of thirteen men, who at this time enlisted, and received each a bounty of a hundred dollars from Athol, but were never assigned to particular regiments, or in actual service, though for obvious reasons they were credited to this town, and helped to fill our quota.

The names of these men are as follows: —

Charles Streeter.	Benjamin M. Twichell, jun.
Silas Fry.	George R. Phelps.
Charles H. Fry.	Zenas W. Lamb.
Edgar Bent.	Walter Wilber.
Joseph Miller.	William McKee.
Albert Miller.	William Twichell, jun.
M. C. Mayo.	

These men went to Worcester with others who were about to enter the service, and were

there examined by, as they supposed, the proper
authorities, and accepted as able-bodied soldiers.
After being sworn in, but before signing any papers, they received their respective bounties of
a hundred dollars each.   As it was desired that
these men should join regiments already in the
field, they were then sent to Camp Day at Cambridge, with the exception of William Twichell,
who remained at Worcester, but was not permitted to join any company that was leaving for
the seat of war, and was finally sent home as one
upon whom the Government had no claim.

At Camp Day, the men were re-examined, and
all (with the exception of Joseph Miller) were
declared unfit for service, and at length were
permitted to return home. Silas Fry was rejected
because he was too old; two or more, because
they were too young; and the others, for various
disabilities; while all were furnished with the
proper certificates. Joseph Miller had permission to come home for the purpose of entering a
company of nine-months' men about to be formed
in Athol but was prevented from so doing at
that time by sickness. Some time after, a Lieutenant Shaw, said to be from Shrewsbury, came to
Athol and notified ten of these men that they
were wanted in Boston; telling some of them
that there was a misunderstanding about their
coming home, and others that the matter of

back pay was to be settled. Mr. Lamb was not notified, Mr. McKee was not found, and Mr. Mayo was not in town. The ten men went to Boston, and were taken by the Lieutenant in charge to the Hancock House. Mr. Wilber at once made known his case to the proper authorities, and was not again molested. Messrs. Fry, Bent, Streeter and William Twichell, were lodged in jail, and, after being handcuffed with a company of desert-ers, were put to work at Fort Independence. There they remained twenty-three days, poorly fed, and shamefully treated in every respect, till finally a friendly surgeon made known their case to the proper authorities, and an order came for their release, when they came home, paying their own expenses.

Messrs. B. M. Twichell, jun., Joseph Miller, Albert Miller, and George R. Phelps were taken on to Washington and from thence to Alexandria, Va., to the camp for recruits. Two or three times they went through the process of being mustered in to receive pay, but never received any, as their names did not appear upon the rolls. At length, upon a proper representation of their case, the Adjutant-General of Massachu-setts and Provost-Marshal obtained their release as men "not in the service;" and they came home, paying their own expenses.

Whether Lieut. Shaw acted in good faith in

his treatment of these men, it is not for those in charge of this record to decide; but that a most grievous wrong was inflicted upon them, there can be no question.

The President of the United States having issued, Aug. 4, 1862, an additional call for three hundred thousand men to serve for the space of nine months, and to be raised by draft, at a town-meeting on the 28th day of August, 1862, action was taken as follows : —

" *Whereas*, By a recent call by the President of the United States, bearing date Aug. 4, 1862, it was ordered that three hundred thousand men be drafted from the enrolled militia of the several States to serve for the term of nine months, of which number the quota of this Commonwealth has been officially declared to be 19,080 men ; and

Whereas, The quotas of the several towns in this Commonwealth have not been assigned and publicly declared ; and

Whereas, The Governor of this Commonwealth has granted permission to the several towns to furnish volunteers for their proportion of men or any part thereof under said call : therefore

Voted, That the selectmen of Athol be authorized, in behalf of the town, to pay a bounty of one hundred dollars to every inhabitant thereof who shall have enlisted since Aug. 22, 1862, or shall hereafter enlist on or before the 2d day of September next, into the service of the United States for said term of nine months, until the number equal to the quota of said town shall be fully made up."

It was also provided that the payment of this bounty should be made when volunteers offering themselves under it should have been mustered into the service by the proper United States authority, and also that no bounty should be paid by this town to any one who had received or was entitled to receive a bounty from any other town or city.

At the same meeting it was

"*Voted*, That the selectmen be authorized to pay to such widows and children who are entitled to such aid the amount of aid paid by the State." Also

"*Voted*, To extend the time of paying said bounty of a hundred dollars until the time the draft shall be made to fill said quota."

Aug. 14, 1862, an additional regulation was issued by the War Department, directing that in the several States the quotas for the counties, and subdivisions of counties, should be apportioned by the governors, so that allowances should be made for all volunteers previously furnished and mustered into service, whose stipulated term of service should not have expired.

Athol had at this time one hundred and seventy-one men who had enlisted and been mustered into service for three years. The quota of this town under the call for three hundred thousand nine-months' men was sixty-one. The seven men who were lacking to fill the number of three-years' men previously called for, the select-men were authorized to supply by enlistments for nine months.

The enthusiasm manifested by the people of Athol while the men were enlisting for nine months' service was very great. Many offered themselves as soldiers who could not be accept-ed because of some physical disability, and the number actually mustered into service under this call was but fifty-two. Each of these re-ceived from the town the promised bounty of a hundred dollars, and an additional private bounty, as will appear from the statements that follows.

The following is a copy of a paper furnished to the committee who had this record in charge.

"At meetings of the citizens of Athol held in the Town Hall, Saturday evening, Aug. 30, and Tuesday evening, Sept. 2, for the purpose of se-curing volunteers to fill the quota of the town under the call of the President for nine-months' men, the following gentlemen subscribed the

5

sums set against their names, as additional bounty to encourage enlistments.

F. F. Amsden	$100	John Wyman	$10
W. H. Amsden	100	George B. Ellinwood	10
A. Harding, jun.	100	Joseph F. Dunbar	10
Laban Morse	10	Edwin Ellis	10
Ozi Kendall	10	John H. Williams	10
C. M. Spooner	10	John Kendall	10
Dexter Aldrich	10	Goodell Goddard	10
J. Smith Cook	10	J. W. Burbeck	10
John Smith	10	A. D. Horr	20
H. D. Adams	5	James Stratton	5
John Wood	5	J. F. Bates	5
John Lewis	5	Ira Bailey	5
L. K. Sprague	10		

Total amount.... $500

The circumstances of the subscription were as
follows: —

At the first-named meeting when forty-two
names had been secured, F. F. Amsden offered
one hundred dollars as a bounty to the next ten
men, and Washington H. Amsden offered one
hundred dollars for the next ten men, which
would make the number sixty-two.

A. Harding, jun. offered one hundred dollars
in addition for the first ten men, and Laban
Morse, Ozi Kendall, Warren H. Amsden, C. M.
Spooner, Dexter Aldrich, J. Smith Cook, John
Smith, John Wyman, George B. Ellinwood and
Joseph F. Dunbar, offered ten dollars each for the
last ten men. At the Tuesday-evening meeting,

the subscription was continued, and on motion of Laban Morse, it was voted that the different subscriptions be paid in, and the sum which remained after paying the twenty dollars additional bounty, should be divided among those who enlisted first. The names of the subscribers were called and they signified their willingness to agree to the proposition of Mr. Morse, with the exception of the following gentlemen who were absent; viz., Mr. Harding, Mr. Kendall, Mr. Dunbar, and Mr. W. H. Amsden. Mr. Addison D. Horr was chosen as a committee to collect and pay over the money. The money was not to be paid until the volunteers were duly mustered into the service of the United States. The above I certify to be a true record of the facts attending the subscription.

JAMES P. LYNDE,

Chairman of the Meetings."

To show how the money raised in this manner was expended, the following certificate of the committee, Mr. Addison D. Horr, is inserted in this place : —

"This is to certify that I have attended to the duties assigned me in collecting and paying out the money subscribed by the foregoing names, and have made the following distribution of the five hundred dollars. Paid

Warren E. Smith,   B. A. French,
Marshall Collins,   William L. Thrower,
Henry D. Southland,   Welcome J. Cleaveland,
James A. Moore,   Adin Oakes,
George W. Drurey, jun.,   George B. Wood,
William A. Judd,   J. O. Gould,
Ozi Oliver,   Freeman G. Perry,
Alfred Goddard,   George McRae,
Thomas Burns,   Peter Stanton,

Each twenty dollars;

David Walker,   William G. Fay,
Aaron H. Holt,   Charles W. Kendall,
Frederic A. Stratton,   A. B. Folsom,
A. V. Dimock,   Levi B. Fay,
E. F. Chase,   George W. Lincoln,
Henry H. Stratton,   Cyrus W. Conant,
A. W. Conant,   Edward P. Clapp,
Harrison Stockwell,   Simeon S. Drurey,
Freeborn R. Fay,   Rufus Putnam,
Arthur N. Judd,   Harlan P. Townsend,
Harding R. Barber,   Otis B. Boutwell,
L. W. Follett,   Enoch T. Lewis,
Daniel Casavant,   George F. Moore,
Adolphus Bangs,   Charles V. Goddard,
John R. Pierce,

Each four dollars and eighty-two cents.

In addition to this money, there was raised at the first meeting forty dollars, and paid over to the following persons, when they put their names on the roll, viz. Lauriston I. King, Freeman H. Walker, Spencer Stockwell, and Charles H. Tyler, each ten dollars; making $499.78 paid out by the committee, and forty dollars by the donors. Total, $539.78.   ADDISON D. HORR,

Committee to collect and pay the money."

All of the soldiers whose names appear in the certificate of Mr. Horr, given above, received each a town bounty of one hundred dollars, when they were mustered into the service of the United States; and Farwell F. Fay Esq., also of Athol, who was chosen Captain of the company to which these men belonged, received at a later period the same bounty.

Company E, of the Fifty-third Regiment of the Massachusetts volunteer militia, was made up of the fifty-one men named in the above certificate from Athol, F. F. Fay Esq., also from Athol, one man from Phillipston, twenty-five men from Royalston, and eighteen men from New Salem. The names of all these will be given in connection with the account of the service of this company.

Authority having been given by the Governor of the Commonwealth to one of the selectmen of Athol to call these men together, and to lead them to the choice of officers to be commissioned the men met in the town-hall of Athol, Sept. 13, 1862. Mr. Addison D. Horr, one of the Athol board of selectmen, presided, when the following officers of the company were chosen:—

Farwell F. Fay, Esq. of Athol, Captain, Benjamin H. Brown of Royalston, first Lieutenant, Varnum V. Vaughan of New Salem, second Lieutenant. This company was recruited by Capt.

5*

Fay; and, on the morning of the day in which his company went into camp, a sword and sash were presented to him in the town-hall in the presence of his company and of a large audience. The money to purchase these was collected by Mr. Charles M. Spooner; and the Hon. Charles Field made the address of presentation. The sword and sash cost forty-five dollars.

This company went into camp at Camp Stevens, Groton Junction, Oct. 1, 1862, as Company E of the Fifty-third Regiment. Some sickness prevailed in the regiment while in Camp Stevens; and Spencer Stockwell of Athol died there. After remaining at Groton Junction two months, the regiment was ordered to New York, and left for that city Nov. 30, 1862. The men suffered much from cold and storms before they reached their temporary home at Franklin-street barracks, New-York City. While there, George B. Wood, from Athol, was discharged on account of sickness and died the day after his discharge. Bernard H. Doane of Company E, from Royalston, being sick, was also discharged before the regiment left for the seat of war; while Charles P. Bliss of New Salem joined the company and was mustered into the service in New York. The number of men in Company E, when the regiment left for the seat of war, was ninety-four; but of these, two, viz. Lauriston I. King of Athol and George H. Wood of Royalston, were left in New York sick.

Dec. 24, 1862, a Christmas dinner was forwarded to Company E from the store of Messrs. Hunt and Packard, Athol. This reached New York in season, and the company dined together on the evening of Dec. 25. As the friends of the company in Royalston had sent a sum of money to the men from that town for a dinner, and as all dined together upon the supplies sent from Athol on Christmas, by invitation of the men from Royalston, all dined together again at the National Hotel, New York, Jan. 1, 1863. Each was an occasion of interest.

The Fifty-third Regiment embarked on board the "Mississippi" for the Gulf of Mexico; but such was the amount of sickness prevailing, that it was not deemed prudent to proceed on the voyage, and all disembarked. But the health of the men being at length in a good degree restored, Jan. 16, 1863, the regiment embarked again on board the steamer "Continental" for New Orleans. After a very stormy passage of twelve days, in which winds, rains, fire and sickness conspired to render the situation of the men uncomfortable and perilous, the regiment reached that city Jan. 31, and went into camp at Carrollton, La., six miles from New Orleans.

Just before Company E went into camp at

Camp Stevens, Groton Junction, viz. on the 18th day of Sept., 1862, at a town-meeting duly called it was

"*Voted*, The selectmen be authorized to pay a bounty of one hundred dollars each to such of the inhabitants of the town who have enlisted into the company of which Farwell F. Fay is elected Captain, as shall be accepted and mustered into the service of the United States."

During the year 1862, eighty-seven families of soldiers received aid under the several acts of the town of Athol recorded on the foregoing pages.

The amount paid by the selectmen to these eighty-seven families was $5,314.49. Of this sum, the amount refunded by the State was $4,102.34, leaving as paid by the town the sum of $1,212.15. The highest amount paid to any family was four hundred and sixteen dollars, which was paid to the family of John O. Mowry of Company B Twenty-seventh Regiment.

The names of the soldiers whose families were thus aided, and the amount received by each family, during the year 1862, were as follows: —

	To aid,	Whole Amount paid.	Refunded by State.
Lewis P. Atwood,	Mother,	$104.00	52.00
Jeduthan W. Ames,	Mother,	38.86	38.86
J. B. Billings,	Mother,	13.14	6.57
John S. Briggs,	Wife & Children,	180.00	83.60
Eli Bodet,	Wife & Children,	144.00	144.00

	To aid,	Whole Amount paid.	Refunded by State.
Francis B. Brock,	Father,	104.00	52.00
Harding R. Barber,	Wife & Child,	21.42	21.42
Joseph Bracewell,	Wife & Children,	54,57	54.57
Adolphus Bangs,	Wife & Child,	21.42	21.42
Thomas Burns,	Wife & Children,	29.60	29.60
Otis B. Boutwell,	Wife,	10.71	10.71
J. B. Cummings,	Wife & Child,	136.28	90.86
John M. Casavant,	Wife & Children,	60.00	60.00
Marshall Collins,	Wife & Child,	21.42	21.42
Joseph II. Collins,	Wife,	104.00	52.00
George II. Clark,	Parents,	84.28	84.28
Warren E. Chamberlain,	Wife & Children,	40.57	40.57
Simeon S. Drurey,	Wife & Mother,	21.42	21.42
Patrick Dempsey,	Wife & Children,	162.00	144.00
II. N. Darling,	Wife & Child,	43.42	43.42
Otis E. Davis,	Wife & Children,	62.40	62.40
John Doyle,	Wife & Children,	56.00	56.00
Azer S. Davis,	Wife & Child,	40.57	40.57
George W. Drurey, jun.,	Wife & Father,	21.42	21.42
A. V. Dimock,	Wife,	10.73	10.73
L. W. Follett,	Wife,	10.73	10.73
William G. Fay,	Wife,	10.73	10.73
Elmer G. Foster,	Mother,	7.42	7.42
A. B. Folsom,	Wife & Children,	29.60	29.60
Patrick W. Fox,	Mother,	104.00	52.00
William A. Fry,	Wife,	52.00	52.00
Charles D. Fisher,	Wife & Child,	40.57	40.57
Daniel W. Foster,	Wife & Child,	43.43	43.43
Silas Fry,	Wife & Children,	60.00	60.00
Byron A. French,	Wife & Child,	21.42	21.42
Freeborn R. Fay,	Wife & Children,	29.60	29.60
Samuel A. Hill,	Wife,	87.40	43.70
Gardner Howe,	Wife & Children,	144.00	144.00
James A. Hand,	Wife & Child,	98.00	98.00
James S. Hodge,	Wife,	144.00	52.00
Aaron II. Holt,	Wife & Children,	29.60	29.60
William H. Johnson,	Mother,	22.28	11.14

	To aid,	Whole Amount paid.	Refunded by State.
Milton N. Jillson,	Wife & Children,	78.74	78.74
William A. Judd,	Wife & Children,	29.60	29.60
Lauriston I. King,	Wife & Child,	21.43	21.43
Charles W. Kendall,	Wife & Children,	29.60	29.60
Fernaldo L. Lord,	Wife & Children,	60.00	60.00
Enoch T. Lewis,	Wife & Child,	21.42	21.42
George W. Meacham,	Wife & Children,	328.42	114.00
Jonathan B. Mills,	Wife,	21.14	21.14
George Morse,	Wife,	26.56	13.28
John O. Mowry,	Wife & Children,	416.00	144.00
George F. Moore,	Mother,	10.70	10.70
Norris B. Meacham,	Wife,	9.50	4.75
Edmond Moore,	Mother,	104.00	52.00
George W. Nelson,	Wife & Child,	100.00	100.00
Adin Oakes,	Wife & Children,	29.60	29.60
Ozi Oliver,	Wife,	10.71	10.71
Rufus Putnam,	Wife & Child,	21.42	21.42
James C. Parker,	Wife & Children,	94.50	74.00
Asa Phillips,	Wife & Children,	65.20	53.60
Foster W. Phelps,	Parents,	104.00	104.00
John R. Pierce,	Wife & Child,	18.00	18.00
James Oliver, 2d	Wife & Child,	40.57	40.57
William Richardson,	Wife & Child,	102.80	68.56
Joshua Rich,	Wife,	20.29	20.29
Neri F. Ripley,	Child,	49.00	49.00
Harvey Robbins,	Wife & Children,	60.00	60.00
James H. Richardson,	Wife & Child,	177.00	128.07
George McRae,	Wife & Children,	29.60	29.60
Charles Sears,	Wife,	21.70	21.70
Harrison Stockwell,	Wife & Child,	21.42	21.42
Emory Sawin,	Wife & Children,	56.00	56.00
Peter Stanton,	Wife & Children,	29.60	29.60
Albert Simonds,	Wife & Children,	50.00	50.00
Warren E. Smith,	Wife & Children,	29.60	29.60
Nathaniel B. Twichell,	Wife & Children,	41.57	41.57
William L. Thrower,	Child,	10.70	10.70
Benjamin M. Twichell, jun.,	Wife,	20.28	20.28
Horace K. Weaver,	Wife & Child,	104.00	104.00

	To aid,	Whole Amount paid.	Refunded by State.
Walter Wilber,	Wife & Children,	56.00	56.00
Nelson G. Wood,	Mother,	21.70	21.70
E. W. Whitney,	Wife & Children,	60.00	60.00
Freeman H. Walker,	Wife,	10.70	10.70
William Washburn,	Wife & Children,	58.40	58.40
Asa Wyman,	Wife & Children,	58.00	58.00
Morgan Young,	Wife,	104.00	52.00

Amos L. Cheney, John Kendall and A. D. Horr were the Selectmen of the Town of Athol for the year commencing March 1862.

The year closed with the Rebellion unsubdued, while nearly all the loyal Regiments in the field of conflict greatly needed recruits.

1863.

The Commonwealth having provided that any City or Town might raise money to continue to pay the State Aid to the families of deceased or disabled soldiers for the space of one year unless pensions should be previously granted to them, at a Town meeting legally called, and held May 9, 1863, it was

"*Voted*, To continue to pay the State Aid to the families of deceased and disabled soldiers, according to the provisions of a recent act of the Legislature."

A Conscription Act having been passed by

Congress for the purpose of recruiting the forces of the United States, a new enrollment of the men liable to military service, was ordered under the authority of the General Government. The enrolling Officer for Athol was Mr. Addison D. Horr, of the Board of Selectmen.

The enrollment was ordered for July 1, 1863; and the enrolled men were to be divided into two Classes.

The first class comprised all between the ages of twenty and thirty-five years and the unmarried men and widowers between thirty-five and forty-five.

The second class comprised the married men, who were more than thirty-five, but under forty-five years of age. Athol was found to have three hundred and six men of the first class, without including any who were at that date in the service of the United States.

The first Draft was ordered to be made from the first class and was made to equal one seventh of the whole, with the addition of fifty per cent. of the same for exemptions. The Quota for Athol was therefore sixty-six; and these were drawn at Greenfield, the Head Quarters of the 9th District, July 14th, 1863.

The names drawn and the results of the examination of the conscripts are here given as follows. The men were drawn in the order observed in making this record of them.

John E. Woods,	Exempted.
Samuel Searls,	do.
Nathan C. Knowlton,	do.
Albert Sanderson,	Accepted. Furnished Substitute.
William N. Gleason,	Exempted.
Emory Gage,	do.
William H. Foster,	do.
C. C. Horr,	Accepted. Furnished Substitute.
Dwight Smith,	Exempted.
Elijah L. Bryant,	Accepted. Furnished Substitute.
George W. Rickey,	Exempted.
Leander W. Phelps,	do.
Jeduthan W. Ames,	do.
J. B. Billings,	do.
Hart L. Keyes,	do.
George B. Ellinwood,	Accepted. Furnished Substitute.
J. Alonzo Whitney,	do. do. do.
F. D. Bullard,	Exempted.
Adoniram J. Fay,	Accepted. Furnished Substitute.
Guilford W. Lamb, jun.,	Accepted. Reported for Service.
James F. Whitcomb,	Accepted. Furnished Substitute.
Daniel D. Bruce,	Accepted. Reported for Service.
Albert H. Lawrence,	Accepted. Furnished Substitute.
W. H. Frost,	Exempted.
John F. Merrill,	do.
Sereno E. Fay,	do.
James S. Jobbins,	do.
G. Sumner Goddard,	Accepted. Furnished Substitute.
James Coolidge,	Exempted.
William M. Leonard,	do.
Frederic N. Brockett,	do.
Branch F. Ayers,	do.
Maxon R. Wetherby,	Accepted. Reported for Service.
Orrin F. Hunt,	Exempted.
John H. Bullard,	do.
Simeon B. Newton,	Accepted. Paid Commutation.
Francis L. Pond,	Exempted.
Ensign A. Marsh,	do.
Lucian Lord,	do.

Sullivan Moore,	Exempted.
Lyman A. Chamberlain,	do.
Warren A. Beaman,	Accepted. Reported for Service.
Horatio Mann,	Accepted. Furnished Substitute.
Hiram L. Reynolds,	Exempted.
Hubbard V. Smith,	do.
David D. Gay,	do.
George Stockwell,	do.
Gardner Howe,	do.
George H. Barry,	do.
George W. Andrews.	do.
Henry W. Stratton,	do.
Amos A. Warrick,	Accepted. Furnished Substitute.
Thomas H. Goodspeed.	Exempted.
John E. Moore,	Accepted. Furnished Substitute.
Lucius R. Sprague,	Exempted.
Edwin F. Williams.	do.
Frederic T. George,	Accepted. Furnished Substitute.
Henry A. Stearns.	Exempted.
Henry Lee,	do.
Henry Kendall,	Accepted. Paid Commutation.
Alonzo E. Pratt,	Exempted.
George P. Sloan,	Accepted. Furnished Substitute.
Benj. M. Twichell, jun.,	Exempted.
George H. Richardson,	do.
Ephraim Rice,	do.
George E. Phelps,	do.

From the above it appears that of the sixty-six men drafted from Athol, only twenty, or a little less than one third, were held to serve. This proportion may seem very small, but it will be found to be considerably larger than the average throughout the Commonwealth. The whole number of men drafted at this time in Massachusetts was 32,079; of these there were held to serve 6,690 or considerably less than one fourth. Of those held to serve only 743 joined the service, while 2,325 procured substitutes and 3,623 paid commutation which amounted to $1,085,800.

The number of men who failed to report was 3,044 and the number of men exempted was 22,343.

Of the twenty men accepted from Athol, as will be seen above, fourteen procured substitutes, two paid the commutation of three hundred dollars each, and four reported for service. Of the four last mentioned, one, Warren A. Beaman was a prisoner at Andersonville Georgia, and died at Annapolis on his way home.

It should be stated here, that the lot that fell upon them was a very expensive thing to the young gentlemen from Athol who procured substitutes or paid commutation. The commutation was three hundred dollars each, while substitutes could not be procured at that time, carried to Greenfield and their expenses paid till they were actually received into the service of the Government without an additional outlay of forty dollars, on an average.

The fourteen Substitutes cost therefore nearly or quite $4,760. The commutation paid was $600, making the amount paid by the sixteen young gentlemen, who in this manner did their part to serve the country, $5,360.

In some cases, it took all, and more than all these men possessed to meet the expenses of this draft; a fact which their fellow-townsmen should hold in perpetual remembrance.

More men being wanted for the service of the Government, another call for troops was issued by the President, Oct. 17, 1863. This call was for three hundred thousand men, and the quota for Athol under it was thirty-three.

Premiums of fifteen dollars each for raw recruits and of twenty-five dollars each for veterans, were offered by the Government, to promote enlistments; but these were in no case to go to the recruits, but to the Agents who might secure them for the service. In Athol, this matter was properly arranged and conducted by the Selectmen who appointed Byron A. French and Patrick W. Fox their assistants. Under this arrangement twenty men were secured for the service of the Government from Athol, one half of whom were veterans, or men who re-entered the service.

Late in the summer of 1863, the surviving members of Company E, Fifty-third Regiment, under Capt. F. F. Fay returned from the South-West to Athol and its vicinity, their term of enlistment having expired. A particular account of their reception &c. will be found under the History of the services of that Regiment, in this Record.

During the year 1863, Seventy-Five families of soldiers from Athol received aid under the several acts of the Town and Commonwealth for the encouragement of enlistments. The amount paid by the Selectmen to these seventy-five families during the year was $7,032.03. Of this sum there was refunded by the State the sum of $6,664.23, leaving as a charge upon the Treasury of the Town $367.80.

The highest sum paid to any family was $197.70: which was paid to the family of John O. Mowry.

The names of the soldiers whose families received State and Town Aid and the amounts paid to each during the year 1863, were as follows: —

	To aid	
Lewis P. Atwood,	Wife,	$104.00
Harding R. Barber,	Wife & Child,	70.00
J. B. Billings,	Mother,	42.00
Warren A. Beaman,	Wife,	19.00
Eli Bodet,	Wife & Children,	124.80
Francis B. Brock,	Father,	56.00
Joseph Bracewell,	Wife & Children,	144.00
Adolphus Bangs,	Wife & Child,	70.00
Thomas Burns,	Wife & Children,	96.80
Otis B. Boutwell,	Wife,	35.00
Marshall Collins,	Wife & Child,	89.00
Joseph H. Collins,	Wife,	42 43
George H. Clark,	Father & Mother,	104.00
Warren E. Chamberlain,	Wife & Child,	104.00
Simeon S. Drurey,	Wife & Mother,	70.00

	To aid	
Welcome J. Cleaveland,	Mother,	52.00
Patrick Dempsey,	Wife & Children,	144.00
Henry N. Darling,	Wife & Children,	142.00
Otis E. Davis,	Wife & Children,	144.00
John Doyle,	Wife & Children,	144.00
Azor S. Davis,	Wife & Child,	104.00
George W. Drurey,	Wife & Father,	70.00
Anthony V. Dimock,	Wife & Child,	66.43
William G. Fay,	Wife,	35.00
Leyton W. Follett,	Wife,	35.00
A. B. Folsom,	Wife & Children,	96.80
Patrick W. Fox,	Mother,	54.85
William A. Fry,	Wife,	52.00
Charles D. Fisher,	Wife & Child,	104.00
Daniel W. Foster,	Wife & Child,	96.57
Byron A. French,	Wife & Children,	81.82
Gardner Howe,	Wife & Children,	142.40
Freeborn R. Fay,	Wife & Children,	96.80
James A. Hand,	Wife & Children,	144.00
James S. Hodge,	Wife,	87.85
Aaron H. Holt,	Wife & Children,	96.80
William H. Johnson,	Mother,	42.00
Milton N. Jillson,	Wife & Children,	144.00
William A. Judd,	Wife & Children,	96.80
Lauriston I. King,	Wife & Child,	70.00
Charles W. Kendall,	Wife & Children,	96.80
Fernaldo L. Lord,	Wife & Children,	144.00
Enoch T. Lewis,	Wife & Child,	70.00
John O. Mowry,	Wife & Children,	197.70
George F. Moore.	Mother,	35.00
Edmond Moore,	Mother,	104.00
Adin Oakes,	Wife & Children,	144.00
Ozi Oliver,	Wife,	35.00
Rufus Putnam,	Wife & Child,	70.00

	To aid	
Albert D. Pond,	Father & Mother,	104.00
Asa Phillips,	Wife & Children,	116.00
Foster W. Phelps,	Father & Mother,	104.00
John R. Pierce,	Wife & Child,	70.00
James Oliver, 2d,	Wife & Child,	104.00
Joshua Rich,	Wife,	52.00
Neri F. Ripley,	Child,	42.00
Harvey Robbins,	Wife & Children,	144.00
James H. Richardson,	Wife & Child,	156.00
George McRae,	Wife & Children,	96.80
Charles Sears,	Wife,	52.00
Harrison Stockwell,	Wife & Child,	70.00
Emory Sawin,	Wife & Children,	144.00
Peter Stanton,	Wife & Children,	96.80
Warren E. Smith,	Wife & Children,	96.80
N. B. Twichell,	Wife & Children,	144.00
William L. Thrower,	Child,	35.00
Albert Simonds,	Wife & Children,	144.00
Horace K. Weaver,	Wife & Child,	104.00
Nelson G. Wood,	Mother,	52.00
E. W. Whitney,	Wife & Children,	144.00
Freeman H. Walker,	Wife & Parents,	105.00
William Washburn,	Wife & Children,	144.00
Asa Wyman,	Wife & Children,	114.28
Maxon R. Wetherby,	Wife & Children,	66.80
Morgan Young,	Wife,	71.14

Total amount as above,..............	$6,983.27
Supplementary account allowed, ...	$56.96
Subtract for error, ...	8.20
Amount corrected,.................	$7,032.03
Of this the State refunded, ...	6,664.23
Paid by the Town,.................	$367.80

Of the last amount the family of

Lewis P. Atwood received............	$52.00
Patrick W. Fox,...............	6.42
James S. Hodge,................	35.71
John O. Mowry,................	130.10
Edmund Moore,................	52.00
James H. Richardson,.............	52.00
Morgan Young,................	35.57

Calvin Kelton Esqr., Mr. A. D. Horr and Mr. Amos L. Cheney were the Selectmen of Athol for the year commencing March 1863.

1864.

Feb. 1, 1864, the President of the United States issued a call for 500,000 troops; it being understood that this number might include

1. All the Drafted men that reported for service, paid the commutation or furnished Substitutes, during the summer of 1863;

2. All who had volunteered and been mustered into the service of the United States after July 1, 1863; and

3. All who having been in the service of the United States with less than one year to serve had re-enlisted or would re-enlist for an additional term of three years or for the war.

Of the first class mentioned above the Town

of Athol had already furnished twenty men, and
of the second class the same number.

Nineteen men from Athol re-enlisted and were
credited to this town, viz.

Asa L. Kneeland.	John Clark.
Ebenezer Kneeland.	Theodore Washburn.
Charles Gray.	Charles C. Phelps.
D. W. Larned.	Thomas Johnson.
A. D. Pond.	William Beard.
N. B. Twichell.	T. A. Woodward.
George D. Townsend.	Willard Twichell.
Delevan Richardson.	Foster W. Phelps.
D. E. Billings.	Fernaldo L. Lord.
Lewis P. Atwood.	

James Connell of Athol re-enlisted but was
held contrary to his written protest by the Town
of Wareham. Prescott M. Metcalf and Levi
Bosworth re-enlisted for Athol but were held by
Royalston. Charles H. Barton re-enlisted and
was credited to Philadelphia, while John Clark
and Theodore Washburn who went originally
from Phillipston were credited to Athol.

The nineteen re-enlistments above mentioned
with the forty men previously obtained filled
the quota from Athol, under the call of Feb. 1,
1864, and left a small surplus, but precisely how
large this was, it is difficult to determine, since
the names of the men who re-enlisted were not
all returned to the Office of the Provost Marshal at Boston till after the 15th of Feb.

March 15, 1864, the President issued another call for 200,000 troops, and the quota of Athol under this call was thirty-two. The surplus of re-enlisted men and twenty-seven other men obtained through Brokers made up this number.

The Legislature of Massachusetts having provided by the Act of March 16, 1864, that cities and Towns might raise money by taxation or otherwise for the purpose of procuring volunteers and pay to each one enlisted into the service as a part of the quota of said Cities or Towns a sum not exceeding one hundred and twenty five dollars, a Town Meeting was called for April 16, 1864, at which it was voted,

"That the Town raise by taxation the sum of Three Thousand Dollars for the purpose of paying under the direction of the Selectmen one hundred and twenty-five Dollars in aid of and for the purpose of procuring each recruit who may be mustered into the United States service from Athol, under the last call of the President of the United States for 200,000 men."

As the sum raised April 16, 1864, was only sufficient to pay the proposed bounties to twenty-four men, and as twenty-seven were required to fill the quota, another Town Meeting was called for June 4, 1864, at which by a vote similar to the above, the additional sum of three hundred and seventy-five Dollars was raised, for the purpose of procuring three additional recruits for Athol.

At the same meeting it was voted

"To raise a sum of money sufficient to pay each man who may volunteer or each enrolled who may furnish a Substitute for said enrolled man, and said volunteer or substitute to be duly mustered into the service of the United States and credited to the Town of Athol, the sum of one hundred and twenty-five dollars each; said sum of money to be paid to any one who may volunteer or furnish a Substitute at any time within three months from the date hereof, provided they are duly mustered and credited to the Town of Athol."

Under this last mentioned vote of the Town, no bounties were paid.

The Twenty-seven men above referred to who completed the quota of Athol under the call of March 15, 1864, received each as a bounty from the Town the sum of one hundred and twenty-five dollars, and from the Citizens of the Town an average additional bounty each, of Fifty-one dollars and Fifty cents.

In July, 1864, the Secretary of War issued an order for the organization of Regiments to serve for 100 days. The men serving in these were to receive no bounty, but were not liable to draft during their term of service. Athol furnished four men under this call.

Another call for 500,000 additional troops was made by the President of the United States July 19, 1864; and at a Town Meeting Aug. 6, 1864, it was

Voted to "raise a sum of money to be paid out under the direction of the Selectmen, in aid of and for the purpose of procuring recruits necessary to fill the whole quota of the Town, under the call of the President of the United States dated July 18, 1864, after deducting the surplus to which the Town was entitled, not exceeding 125 dollars for each recruit." It was also

"Voted that the Selectmen be authorized to deposit such sum of money authorized to be raised by the above vote, with the State Treasurer, as they may deem best and necessary, for the purpose of obtaining recruits from States in rebellion, in accordance with an order from the Governor of the Commonwealth." Under the last vote above the Selectmen deposited in the State Treasury the sum of 1000 Dollars a part of which at a later period was used for the purpose indicated and obtained three recruits who were credited to Athol; and the sum remaining was withdrawn.

Under the call of July 19, 1864, six men enlisted from Athol for the term of one year, and twenty-five other men were obtained through Brokers. Of the last mentioned, four enlisted for one year, one for two years, and the other twenty for three years.

Each of these thirty-one men received a Town Bounty of 125 Dollars, while the additional amount paid for each by the citizens of Athol averaged $236.13.

Upon a careful review of the accounts kept in the Office of the Provost Marshal at Boston Sept. 19, 1864, it appeared that Athol had, under all the previous calls a surplus of seven men. At a later period one was added to this number making the surplus at the time the next call was issued, eight men.

Dec. 19, 1864, the President called for 300,000 additional troops, and under this call the quota for Athol was thirty-six.

At a Town Meeting Dec. 31, 1864, it was voted, as under previous calls, to raise and appropriate a sum sufficient to pay each recruit requisite to fill this quota, 125 Dollars.

The quota was filled as follows. Credited to the Town as stated above, eight. Obtained by enlistments here and through Brokers, twenty-four. Representative recruits, four; making a total of thirty-six men. Of the 24 men named above, five enlisted for one year each, and the remaining nineteen for three years each. The Town paid for each of these a bounty of 125 dollars, while the additional bounty paid by the

7

citizens of Athol was for each, on an average, as follows.   For the three years men $139.47.   For the one year men $52.00.

The Representative recruits, for each of whom the requisite sum had been deposited in the State Treasury were as follows —

Private John Mier   For C. C. Bassett Esqr.
   "   Dennis Caldwell   "   Asa Hill.
   "   Daniel Bruce   "   Calvin Kelton Esqr.
   "   Moses Wilkinson   "   Lewis Thorpe.

And to these at a later period were added Private William Freeman for Walter Thorpe, and Henry Williams for David F. Wood.   It is stated in the Adjutant General's Report, that the surplus of Athol under all the calls previous to Dec. 1, 1864, was ten men.   We have the same authority for stating that after the quota of Athol under the last call viz. that of Dec. 19, 1864, was filled, the Town had a surplus of twenty-eight men.

It should be noted in this place that in the distribution among the towns and cities of the Commonwealth of the men in the Naval Service of the United States, who had been credited to the State of Massachusetts, and not to any particular town or city therein, Athol was credited with fifteen men, in addition to the four we already had in the Navy.   Of course, the names of these fifteen men do not appear upon this Record.

As the history of recruiting for the United States service in Athol properly closes with the end of the year 1864, the following summary of the results may here be presented.

In this record there will be found the names of Three Hundred and Thirty-Five men, whom Athol furnished to aid in suppressing the Great Rebellion. Of these, nineteen re-enlisted, and these of course were counted twice in filling our quotas. Seventeen others of the 335 re-entered the service after recovering from the wounds or sickness on account of which they had been discharged. This number includes four Musicians who were discharged by an Order discontinuing Regimental Bands of Music.

To these we add the fifteen credited to Athol through the enlistments of Massachusetts men in the Navy. The whole number furnished by the Town to fill quotas was therefore 386. And to this amount we are to add one man for whom the Provost Marshal gives us credit but of whom we can give no account and we have the sum total 387.

During the year 1864 Seventy-Four families of soldiers received aid under the several acts of the Town and State to encourage enlistments.

In the case of the family of William Washburn, aid was received after his death under the name of his son Oscar Washburn.

The names of the soldiers whose families were thus aided, and the amounts received by each, were as follows —

NAMES.	To aid	Amount.
Lewis P. Atwood,	Wife,	$52.00
J. W. Ames,	Mother,	39.71
D. E. Billings,	Mother,	52.00
W. A. Beaman,	Wife & Child,	95.00
Eli Bodet,	Widow & Children,	24.00
Francis B. Brock,	Father,	52.00
Joseph Bracewell,	Wife & Children,	132.00
John S. Brown,	Wife & Children,	140.00
Daniel D. Bruce,	Father,	52.00
Joseph H. Collins,	Wife,	8.00
Horatio W. McClellan,	Mother,	52.00
Marshall Collins,	Child,	8.00
George H. Clark,	Father & Mother,	104.00
W. E. Chamberlain,	Wife & Child,	16.00
John Clark,	Wife,	39.14
L. A. Chamberlain,	Mother,	31.00
James Cotton,	Wife & Child,	35.98
Patrick Dempsey,	Wife & Children,	68.40
Henry N. Darling,	Wife & Children,	106.80
Otis E. Davis,	Wife & Children,	144.00
John Doyle,	Wife & Children,	144.00
Azor S. Davis,	Wife & Child,	84.00
Terrence Donelly,	Mother,	34.57
William Donelly,	Wife,	22.57
Patrick W. Fox,	Mother,	52.00
William A. Fry,	Wife,	47.14
Charles D. Fisher,	Wife & Child,	92.56

Daniel W. Foster,	Wife & Child,	16.00
Gardner Howe,	Wife & Children,	28.80
James A. Hand,	Wife & Children,	122.00
James S. Hodge,	Widow,	35.85
Edwin C. Hastings,	Wife & Child,	104.00
John W. Howe,	Wife,	52.00
Joseph W. Howard,	Mother,	39.42
Michael J. Hudson.	Wife & Child,	35.14
William H. Johnson,	Mother,	10.00
Milton N. Jillson,	Wife & Children,	144.00
Ebenezer Kneeland,	Wife,	48.00
Lauriston I. King,	Widow & Child,	87.71
Fernaldo L. Lord,	Wife & Children,	144.00
Irving N. Leonard,	Father,	17.57
George W. Meacham,	Wife & Children,	144.00
Edmund Moore,	Mother,	77.43
James Oliver, 2d,	Wife & Child,	77.43
Adin Oakes,	Widow & Children,	36.00
Albert D. Pond,	Father,	52.00
Foster W. Phelps,	Parents,	104.00
Charles C. Phelps,	Wife,	26.00
Peter Pelkey,	Wife & Children,	144.00
Asa Phillips,	Widow & Children,	28.00
John Plunkett,	Wife & Child,	71.71
Chauncey Parkman, jun.,	Child,	52.00
Charles Kent, jun.,	Mother,	34.42
Joshua Rich,	Widow,	52.00
N. F. Ripley,	Child,	10.00
Harvey Robbins,	Widow & Children,	48.00
James H. Richardson,	Wife & Child,	114.00
W. J. Rogers,	Wife,	21.85
Charles Sears,	Wife,	38.43
Emory Sawin,	Wife & Children,	144.00
Albert Simonds.	Wife & Children,	106.80
George W. Stevens.	Mother,	24.00

7*

Peter Stanton,	Wife & Children,	18.00
N. B. Twichell,	Wife & Children,	144.00
Horace O. Thayer,	Mother,	52.00
George D. Townsend,	Wife,	13.00
Horace K. Weaver,	Wife & Child,	94.57
Nelson G. Wood,	Mother,	52.00
E. W. Whitney,	Wife & Children,	90.00
William Washburn.	Wife & Children,	98.00
Oscar Washburn,	Mother.	16.71
Asa Wyman,	Children,	104.00
Maxon R. Wetherby,	Wife & Children,	130.92
Theodore Washburn,	Mother,	39.14
Henry N. Smith.	Wife & Children,	144.00

Total Amount paid $5011.58
Leaving paid by the Town after the State
   had refunded.................... 4941.86

the sum of $69.72
Viz. on account of Edmund Moore $38.72
And of James H. Richardson 31.00

The Selectmen of Athol for the year commencing March 1864 were Calvin Kelton Esqr, Josiah Haven and Gardner Lord Jr.

1865.

Seven of the soldiers obtained by Athol to fill the call for troops made Dec. 19, 1864, were not mustered into the service till early in the Year 1865.

The year opened with encouraging prospects of the speedy and total suppression of the Rebellion. No new troops were called for, while Maj. Gen. Sherman, with an invincible army, was laying waste Georgia and the Carolinas, and Maj. Gen. Grant's movements were filling Richmond, the rebel Capital, with consternation. April 2, the rebel Government fled from Richmond, and the next morning the city was occupied by Gen. Grant's Army. The remnant of Gen. Lee's army was surrendered to Gen. Grant after a few days of desperate fighting, and in an incredibly short space of time the Rebellion was suppressed and the Confederacy had vanished.

Early in the year, our soldiers began to return to their homes, and long before its close but few remained in the field. The sacrifices of the Town of Athol to maintain this mighty conflict with treason have been great. The men who have died in the service or from diseases contracted in it, from the Town of Athol number at least fifty and perhaps fifty-one. Of this number there were killed or died of wounds received in action fourteen. There died of various diseases thirty-four. Killed by cars, one. Thrown from a horse one. Total Fifty.

Four died while prisoners at Andersonville Ga. viz. S. E. Oliver, Samuel Rich, John W. Howe, Geo. S. Dresser, and probably E. R. West.

One died just after leaving Andersonville, viz. Warren A. Beaman.

Twenty-Eight men from Athol were in rebel prisons for a longer or shorter period. Of those who were severely wounded and have wholly or in part recovered there were thirty-one, and some of these were wounded on two or more occasions or in two or more places, — while the number of those slightly wounded was about the same.

Martin L. Maynard of the 36th Regiment lost a leg in the service, and he is the only soldier from Athol known to have been permanently disabled by the loss of a limb.

A particular account of these sufferings and losses will be found under the head, "Personal History of the Athol Soldiers and seamen in the War," contained in the latter part of this Record.

During the year 1865 fifty-seven families of soldiers furnished by Athol received aid under the several acts of the Town and State to encourage enlistments. The names of these soldiers and the amounts received by their respective families were as follows.

	To aid	
Lewis P. Atwood,	Wife,	$10.28
Jeduthan W. Ames,	Mother,	20.00
David E. Billings,	Mother,	27.86
Warren A. Beaman,	Wife & Child,	72.00

Francis B. Brock,	Father,	22.00
Daniel D. Bruce,	Father,	21.28
Charles H. Barney,	Wife & Children,	50.00
H. W. McClellen,	Mother,	24.57
George H. Clark,	Parents,	99.43
John Clark,	Wife,	24.43
James Cotton,	Wife & Child,	48.00
Otis E. Davis,	Wife & Children,	66.40
John Doyle,	Wife & Children,	68.80
Terrence Donelly,	Mother,	34.00
William Donelly,	Wife,	24.57
James Eagan,	Mother,	45.43
Patrick W. Fox,	Mother,	33.71
Joseph Falvey,	Mother,	47.14
M. E. Guilfoyle,	Wife & Children,	70.40
Irving C. Gates,	Mother,	45.14
Edwin C. Hastings,	Wife & Child,	104.00
John W. Howe,	Wife,	26.57
Joseph W. Howard,	Mother,	52.00
Michael J. Hudson,	Wife & Child,	48.00
Milton N. Jillson,	Wife & Children,	48.00
Edwin Holmes,	Mother,	26.00
Ebenezer Kneeland,	Wife & Child,	40.51
Lauriston I. King,	Wife & Child,	16.29
F. L. Lord,	Wife & Children,	66.00
Irving L. Leonard,	Father,	24.00
George W. Meacham,	Wife & Children,	144.00
Frederic P. Morse,	Wife & Child,	11.14
Albert D. Pond,	Father,	25.43
Foster W. Phelps,	Parents,	52.00
Peter Pelkey,	Wife & Children,	86.80
John Plunkett,	Wife & Child,	104.00
Chancey Parkman, Jr.,	Child,	22.00
Charles Kent, Jr.,	Mother,	34.00
Charles C. Phelps,	Wife,	25.57

Francis Powers,	Father,	33.00
Joshua Rich,	Wife,	18.00
Patrick Reardon,	Wife & Child,	61.71
James H. Richardson,	Child,	2.57
William J. Rogers,	Wife & Child,	38.43
Emory Sawin,	Wife & Children,	88.40
Henry N. Smith,	Wife & Children,	90.40
William Smith,	Mother,	25.86
John E. Shattuck,	Mother,	45.14
Nathaniel B. Twichell,	Wife & Children,	36.00
Horace O. Thayer,	Mother,	4.71
George D. Townsend,	Wife,	23.71
Thomas Thompson,	Wife & Children,	125.60
Nelson G. Wood,	Mother,	18.42
Oscar Washburn,	Mother,	8.00
Asa Wyman,	Children,	35.14
Maxon R. Wetherby,	Wife & Child,	48.00
Theodore Washburn,	Mother,	23.72

Whole Amount...................... $2538.62

All of which it is supposed will be refunded by the State.

HISTORICAL NARRATIVE.

Company B 27th Regiment Mass. Volunteers.   Additional particulars.

Names of the original members and of the recruits of 1862.

Captain, Adin W. Caswell.

1st Lieut. P. W. McManus.   Transferred to Comp. I and afterwards Adjutant and a Prisoner.

1st Lieut. W. A. Goodale.   Transferred from Comp. I.

1st Lieut. F. C. Wright.   Promoted from Comp. G.

2d Lieut. Lovell H. Horton.   Resigned 1862.

2d Lieut. Ira B. Sampson.   Capt. 2d Artillery 1863.

Non-Commissioned Officers in 1861.

Sergeant Henry S. Benjamin. Discharged Sept. 1862.
" Henry E. Ballou. Discharged Feb. 1863.
" Charles Grey. Served 3 years. Re-enlisted and was a prisoner.
" Otis Oliver, Wounded and transferred to Invalid Corps, Aug. 1863.
" Daniel W. Larned. See Personal History.
Corporal W. H. Sprague. Died May 1862.
" Mark Rankin. Sergeant Sept. 1862.
" Henry H. Bush. Sergeant Aug. 1863.
" John O. Mowry. See Personal History.
" Van Buren French. See Personal History.
" John R. Morse. See Personal History.
" William H. Pierce. Wounded and Prisoner.
" George V. Oakes. Sergeant 1863.

Musicians.

Addison Leach.
James S. Hodge. Killed by Cars. Sept. 1863.
Wagoner, James P. Little.
Horace B. Allen. Discharged Sept. 1862.
Andrew J. Ames. Transf. to Comp. K. Died April 1862.
Daniel Bosworth. Discharged Oct. 1862.
Levi Bosworth. Corp. 1862. Serg. 1863. Prisoner.
Thomas G. Barry, Discharged Sept. 1862. Died Oct. 1862.
John Bolles, Corp. 1863. Prisoner 1864.
Daniel Blair, Prisoner 1864.
Hiram Blair, Prisoner 1864.
George Britton. Wounded March 1862.
W. B. Bliss, Wounded 1864.
John T. Bliss, Prisoner 1864.
John S. Briggs. See Personal History.
Joseph Bracewell. Prisoner. See Personal History.
William A. Brizzee, Recruit of 1862. Wounded 1864.

John W. Brizzee, Transferred to Comp. C, 1864.

Harry R. Blackner.   See Personal History.

George W. Beard.   Recruit of 1862.

Joseph Briggs, Recruit of 1862.   Wounded severely 1864.

Wm. E. Caswell, Corp. 1863.

Linus Crawford.   See Personal History.

Lyman A. Chamberlain.   See Personal History.

Jason G. Cummings, Discharged Oct. 1862.

John Clark.   See Personal History.

Miles S. Cushing, Recruit 1862.   Died July 1862.

W. N. Dexter, Prisoner 1864.

Joseph Drake, Killed at Newbern March 1862.

Charles Davis, Prisoner 1864.

Frederic S. Day.

Henry N. Darling, Recruit, 1862.

Dwight Freeman.

Frederic L. Fuller.

Harrison E. Goodnow, Transferred to Invalid Corps 1863.

Oseolo Goodnow.

George Gilmore, Wounded at Petersburg 1864.

John W. Gilmore, Died April 1862.

Edwin A. Giles, Transferred to Invalid Corps 1863.

Willard Hodgeman. Discharged Sept. 1862.

William P. Huntoon.

William Hill, Killed 1862.   See Personal History.

Hiram M. Huse. Died Feb. 1864.

George F. Jackson.

D. W. Joslyn.

L. S. Jillson, Died at Roanoke, Feb. 1862.

Milton N. Jillson, Wounded May 1864.

James Kelley.   See Personal History.

Alvin King, Wounded May 1864.

George L. Kendall, Recruit of 1862.

F. X. Lamore, Died Nov. 1862.

Fernaldo L. Lord, Recruit 1862.   See Personal History.

James Miller, Prisoner May 1864.

Prescott M. Metcalf, Corp. June 1863. Prisoner.

Edmund Moore. See Personal History.

Alonzo Murdock, Detailed for Signal Corps.

Geo. W. Meacham. See Personal History.

Norris B. Meacham. See Personal History.

George A. Martin, Discharged April 1862.

George Morse, See Personal History.

George D. Mason, Discharged Aug. 1862.

Patrick M. McGowen, Died Dec. 1861.

Horatio W. McClellen, Corp. June 1863. See P. History.

S. E. Oliver. See Personal History.

Franklin Oliver, Jr. See Personal History.

James Oliver 2d, Recruit of 1862. See Personal History.

Dexter Oakes.

Alphonso Oakes, Discharged Jan. 1864.

William H. Oakes, Died Jan. 1862.

Howard L. Procter, Wounded at Newbern.

Isaac Powers, Wounded March 1862. Died April 1863.

Emory A. Peckham. See Personal History.

Albert D. Pond. See Personal History.

Adin P. Pierce, Discharged March 1863.

J. Henry Packard. See Personal History.

Foster W. Phelps. See Personal History.

Adolphus Porter, Wounded March 1862. Disch. Sept. 1862

Hosea B. Rice, Discharged April 1862.

Charles Reynolds, Died Dec. 1861.

Henry L. Rawson.

James H. Richardson. See Personal History.

Samuel Rich. See Personal History.

Loren Ramsdell.

Harvey Robbins, Recruit 1862. See Personal History.

Forbes Stone.

Dwight Stone.

William H. Stone, Recruit of 1862.

8

Jason Stoddard. Transferred to Invalid Corps Aug. 1863.

J. C. Smith. Discharged April 1863.

Henry D. Steward, Discharged Oct. 1862.

John B. Slate, Wounded June 1864. Recruit.

Henry Smith, Recruit 1862. See Personal History.

Charles Stebbins, Recruit 1862.

Charles Sears, Recruit 1862. See Personal History.

Albert Simonds, Recruit 1862. See Personal History.

Lauriston A. Thorpe. See Personal History.

Robert W. Thrower, Died March 1862. See Personal History.

George D. Townsend, Corp. 1862. See Personal History.

Asa Tilden, Recruit 1862, Prisoner 1864.

N. B. Twichell, Recruit 1862, Corp. 1863. See P. History.

Alonzo J. Thomas, Wounded May 1864.

Amos Upham, Discharged Aug. 1862.

George Ward, Discharged Oct. 1862.

George M. Williams. Discharged Aug. 1862.

Theodore Washburn, See Personal History.

Dexter B. Washburn, Trans. to Comp. E. Oct. 1861.

William H. Whipple, Discharged April 1862.

George M. Whitney, Wounded, Discharged Oct. 1862.

Horace W. Whitaker, Discharged Oct. 1862.

Henry Weeks, Discharged Sept. 1862.

Levi W. Wood, Quarter Master Sergeant Jan. 1863.

E. W. Whitney, Recruit 1862. See Personal History.

Wesley A. Woodward, Recruit 1862. Prisoner 1864.

Ebenezer Winslow, Recruit 1862. Wounded May 1864.

Nelson G. Wood Killed. See Personal History.

Recruits of 1864.

James H. Allen, Prisoner May 1864.

Thomas Barber, Wounded June 1864.

James L. Bragdon. Prisoner May 1864.

John R. Burgess, Veteran.

John M. Dodge, Prisoner May 1864.

George S. Dresser, Prisoner. See Personal History.

Theodore E. Galer, Prisoner May 1864.

Daniel L. Gardner.

George H. Dodge, Killed June 1864.

Charles D. Gilmore.

G. Holenbeck, Prisoner May 1864.

John W. Howe, Prisoner. See Personal History.

Reuben Huntoon, Veteran. Prisoner May 1864.

Moses M. Huse.

Norman Kline.

Martin O. Makley.

L. W. Mason.

Aaron Oliver. See Personal History.

Frank Smith.

James H. Trask.

George E. Trask.

Oscar Washburn. See Personal History.

Charles W. Wheeler Jr., Killed May 1864.

Charles E. Wright, Prisoner May 1864.

Justus Lyman became 2d Lieutenant and was taken Prisoner May 1864.

1st. Lieutenant Frederic C. Wright received a death wound June 5, 1864 while standing by the side of Capt. Caswell.

Mark Rankin 1st Sergeant was taken Prisoner May 1864, so were Sergeants Charles Gray, Levi Bosworth and Henry H. Bush. Also at the same time Corporals John Bolles and W. P. Huntoon were taken prisoners and twenty-three Privates, whose names appear above.

Of the thirty men taken prisoners May 1864, eight were from Athol viz, Charles Gray, Joseph

Bracewell, George S. Dresser, John W. Howe, N.
B. Meacham, S. E. Oliver, Samuel Rich and James
II. Richardson. Of these eight men one half,
viz, Messrs Dresser, Howe, Oliver and Rich died
at Andersonville Ga. of cruel treatment and
starvation, while Messrs Meacham and Richardson but just survived their long imprisonment.
How many of their comrades from Company B
shared the same fate is unknown.

After Company B had been in service more
than two years, 24 men belonging to it, re-en-
listed for the additional term of three years or
for the war, Viz, Hiram Blair, Levi Bosworth,
John W. Brizzee, John Clark, Charles Gray, W.
P. Huntoon, Hiram M. Huse, Daniel W. Joslyn,
Alvin King, D. W. Larned, Addison Leach, F. L.
Lord, II. W. McClellen, P. M. Metcalf, James Miller, Dexter Oakes, A. D. Pond, Henry L. Rawson,
John B. Slate, Henry Smith, Asa Tilden, George
D. Townsend, N. B. Twichell and Theodore
Washburn. As a part of Gen. Burnside's Command, Company B of the 27th Regiment was
first under fire at the Capture of Roanoke Island
N.C. Feb. 8, 1862, and next at the capture of
Newbern. In the latter engagement the Regiment lost 15 killed and 78 wounded. The be-
havior of the men, in these, its early engagements was good. Company B engaged in the
expedition to Hamilton N.C. and was absent,

making forced marches, 14 days. At Rawle's Mills, it was held in reserve. In Dec. 1862, it took part in the expedition to Goldsboro' N.C. and fought the battles of Kinston, White Hall and Goldsboro'. In Jan. 1863, it was sent to Washington N.C., and was one of the two Companies that garrisoned the block-houses on the Greenville and Plymouth roads. In the latter part of March, the famous siege of Washington N.C. commenced, and this lasted 17 days. The force of the rebels was greatly superior to ours, but all its efforts to capture the place were baffled. The weather was cold and rainy, and our troops had but a small supply of rations and ammunition, but they lay in the trenches night and day, and the whole Regiment lost but one killed and eight wounded. The siege having been raised and some of the enemy having been captured in the pursuit, Company B returned to Newbern. Our men were next engaged in the expedition to Batchelder's Creek, and this was followed in May by the successful fight at Gum Swamp. After making a number of less important excursions in North Carolina, the 27th Regiment was ordered to Newport News, Va. and formed a part of Heckman's Brigade. Company B remained some time at Norfolk as Provost-guard, and while there the re-enlisted men came home on a furlough of 30 days. In April 1864,

8*

our men took part in an expedition beyond Suffolk, Va. and returned in a furious snow storm. In May the Regiment was in Yorktown and the knapsacks and all superfluous baggage were sent back to Portsmouth Va. for safe keeping. Our troops were soon sent up the James River and landed at Bermuda Hundred. In the battle at Port Walthall the 27th Regiment had the advance, and the enemy suffered severely. The heat at that time was intense and there were 150 cases of sun-stroke in the Brigade in a single day.

May 9th the 27th Regiment was again in the advance as our troops moved towards Petersburg Va. At Arrowfield Church, the enemy were encountered and made a desperate but, to them, fatal charge upon our lines. Company B lost three of the four men that were killed at that time. May 15th near Drury's Bluff, the 27th Regiment was hard at work constructing breastworks of logs, rails and dirt, with only a dozen shovels, while firing was constantly going on.

May 16, a heavy fog prevailing, the enemy made a furious attack; and it was so difficult to tell friend from foe, that the 27th Regiment was unexpectedly surrounded and a large part of it captured. Of the 252 men of this Regiment that were made prisoners, thirty belonged to Company B. Their names have been already given. Capt. Caswell was sick at the time of this disaster, but June 3, was in the battle at Coal Harbor. In this engagement a piece of a shell struck him between his shoulders, which knocked him down, but in 15 minutes he was able to take command of the Regiment, Major Walker having been killed. The fighting and the marches at that time were terrible. The enemy was desperate while the dust and the stench from dead men and dead horses, was intolerable. In front of Petersburg our men were in the trenches during the hottest weeks of the summer and constantly under fire. In Sept. 1864, the remnant of the Regiment went to Norfolk, Va., and on the 27th of that month those whose term of service had expired were mustered out and returned home. The other part of the Regiment returned to North Carolina, and after various services in that State was engaged in another desperate engagement near Kinston. In this battle, which was followed by the capture of that place, the 27th Regiment with the 15th Connecticut Regiment became separated from the other troops, and nearly all in the two Regiments were taken prisoners. Ten officers and 179 enlisted men of the 27th were captured and enough of the Connecticut troops to make the whole loss 26 officers and 940 men. The prisoners were taken to Weldon N.C. and

from thence to Richmond, having been previously robbed of their money and clothing. At
Richmond they were furnished with food and
clothing by Capt. Stewart of the 146th N. York
Regiment, who had been released to attend to
the wants of our men. These prisoners were
paroled for exchange and reached Annapolis
March 27th 1865. Of Company B three were
severely wounded in the engagement which resulted so disastrously, near Kinston, viz.: Acting
2d Lieut. D. W. Larned, F. L. Lord and John
Clark. These have all recovered. The Rebellion having been effectually suppressed early in
April, the services of the 27th Regiment were no
longer needed and in June 1865, the men composing it were mustered out and returned
home.

Before the three years for which the men
originally enlisted, had expired, Company B had
been in eleven battles and four skirmishes beside
being under constant picket fire, with frequent
shelling for 90 days in Virginia and 17 days in
North Carolina. In all these engagements with
the enemy and under this fire for 107 days Company B lost six killed and 24 wounded. Four of
the 24 were wounded twice or more each. Nine
of these wounds were severe and the remaining
nineteen were slight. George H. Dodge, Joseph
Drake, William Hill, N. B. Twichell, Charles W.

Wheeler and Nelson G. Wood were killed in battle or died soon after from wounds received.

Twenty others died of various diseases or casualties during the three years covered by the original enlistment, viz. :

Horatio R. Blackmer, of Small Pox.
M. S. Cushing, of Consumption.
J. W. Gilmore, of Fever.
W. A. Goodale, of Putrid Sore throat.
J. S. Hodge, Killed by cars.
H. M. Huse, Small Pox.
L. S. Jillson, Fever.
F. X. Lamore, Chronic Diarrhea.
H. W. McClellen, of Scarlatina.
P. McGowan, of Measles.
W. H. Oakes, of Fever.
Isaac Powers, killed by a fall.
Charles Reynolds, of Measles.
Harvey Robbins, of Fever.
W. H. Sprague, of Consumption.
Robert W. Thrower, of Fever.
Samuel Rich, Prisoner, of Chronic Diarrhea.
Sylvanus E. Oliver, Prisoner, of Chronic Diarrhea.
John W. Howe, Prisoner, of Chronic Diarrhea.
George S. Dresser, Prisoner, of Chronic Diarrhea.

How many others of the Company died like the four last mentioned in rebel prisons it is impossible to say.

Three of the six killed and nine of the twenty dying of diseases or accidents were from Athol.

One hundred and sixty men, including recruits,

belonged to Company B, during the three years of the original enlistment.

The sanitary and moral condition of Company B, from first to last, was excellent, and this was due in no small degree to the care and energy of Capt. Caswell in enforcing the rules of sobriety and temperance. A braver Company, it is believed, did not enter the service, for never were these men found wanting.

Company E, 53d Regiment, Mass. Volunteer Militia. Enlisted to serve for nine months.
Additional particulars.
This Company was constituted as follows. Farwell F. Fay, Athol, Captain. See Personal History. B. H. Brown, Royalston, 1st Lieutenant. Varnum V. Vaughan, New Salem, 2d Lieut.

Byron A. French Athol, 1st Sergeant.
Alfred T. King Phillipston, 2d Sergeant.
Adriel C. White Royalston, 3d Sergeant.
David Hamilton Jr. New Salem, 4th Sergeant.
Enoch T. Lewis Athol, 5th Sergeant.
Alonzo French Royalston 1st Corporal.
Edward F. Stratton New Salem 2d Corporal.
Levi B. Fay Athol 3d Corporal.
George W. Warner New Salem 4th Corporal.
Freeman G. Perry Athol 5th Corporal.
Emerson E. Bissell Royalston 6th Corporal.
George W. Knights Royalston 7th Corporal.

Frederic A. Stratton Athol 8th Corporal.

Jerry C. Haskins New Salem Musician.

Privates.

Horace W. Andrews, New Salem,   Sick 3 months.

Charles H. Bliss New Salem.   Died July 1863.

Francis H. Bliss New Salem.   In the battles.

Charles P. Bliss New Salem.   In the battles.

Harding R. Barber Athol, See Personal History.

Adolphus Bangs Athol, See Personal History.

Thomas Burns Athol, See Personal History.

Otis B. Boutwell Athol, See Personal History.

Willis H. Barton Royalston.   In Hospital 4 months.

Amos B. Bosworth Royalston. In Hospital 4 months.

Joseph W. Bosworth Royalston.   Sick.   Discharged.

Ephraim F. Chase Athol, See Personal History.

Cyrus W. Conant Athol, See Personal History.

Artemas W. Conant Athol, See Personal History.

Edmond P. Clapp Athol, See Personal History.

David Casavant Athol, See Personal History.

Marshall Collins Athol, See Personal History.

Welcome J. Cleaveland Athol, See Personal History.

Edward W. Cross Royalston.   Wounded at Port Hudson.

Anthony V. Dimock Athol.   See Personal History.

Simeon S. Drury Athol.   See Personal History.

George W. Drury Jr. Athol.   See Personal History.

Uri C. Day Royalston.   Died April 1863.

Bernard H. Doane Royalston.   Sick.   Discharged Jan. 1863.

Edward M. Ellis New Salem.   Prisoner 2 weeks.

William G. Fay Athol.   See Personal History.

Freeborn R. Fay Athol.   See Personal History.

Azro B. Folsom Athol.   See Personal History.

Leyton W. Follett Athol.   See Personal History.

Martin Falan, Royalston.   Served in all engagements.

Charles Fisher, New Salem.   Sick 4 months.

John K. Freeman, New Salem.   Sick 3 months.

Jacob O. Gould Athol. See Personal History.

Alfred Goddard Athol. See Personal History.

Charles V. Goddard Athol. See Personal History.

Reuben Gibson, New Salem. Sick. In Hospital.

Aaron H. Holt, Athol. See Personal History.

George L. Hancock, Royalston. Died March 1863.

James N. Hunt, Royalston. Served in health.

William A. Judd, Athol. See Personal History.

Arthur N. Judd, Athol. See Personal History.

Charles W. Kendall, Athol. See Personal History.

Lauriston I. King, Athol. See Personal History.

George W. Lincoln, Athol. See Personal History.

George F. Moore, Athol. See Personal History.

James A. Moore, Athol. See Personal History.

John S. Moore, Royalston. Prisoner from June 23 to July 9.

Henry C. Moore, Royalston. Died at New Orleans April 1862.

George W. Morgan Royalston. Wounded at Port Hudson June 1863.

George McRae, Athol. See Personal History.

Andrew J. Norcross, Royalston. Sick 4 months.

Adin Oakes, Athol. See Personal History.

Ozi Oliver, Athol. See Personal History.

Freeman G. Perry, Athol. Corporal 1862. See Personal History.

Rufus Putnam Athol. See Personal History.

Walter T. Putnam, New Salem. Killed at Port Hudson.

Herman M. Partridge, Royalston. Quarter Master Sergeant.

Asa L. Palmer, Royalston. Detailed as Blacksmith.

James L. Powers, New Salem. Sick after June 1863.

John R. Pierce, Athol. See Personal History.

George O. Richardson, Royalston. Furlough 30 days, did not return.

George W. Russell, Royalston. Served in all engagements.

Henry H. Stratton, Athol. See Personal History.

Harrison Stockwell, Athol. See Personal History.

Spencer Stockwell, Athol. See Personal History.

Warren E. Smith, Athol. See Personal History.
Henry S. Smith, New Salem. Died May, 1863.
Elbridge L. Smith, New Salem. Died July 1863.
Henry H. Southland, Athol. See Personal History.
Peter Stanton, Athol. See Personal History.
W. W. Sherwin, Royalston. Sick after fall of Port Hudson.
Harlan P. Townsend, Athol. See Personal History.
Charles H. Tyler, Athol. See Personal History.
William L. Thrower, Athol. See Personal History.
Warren Thatcher, Royalston.
Charles E. Tenney, Royalston. Died April 1863.
Abner E. Towne New Salem. Died July, 1863.
David Walker, Athol. See Personal History.
Freeman H. Walker, Athol. See Personal History.
George B. Wood, Athol. See Personal History.
John M. Wood, Royalston. Died May 1863.
George H. Wood, Royalston. Left sick at New York, Jan. 1863.

Commissioned and Non-Commissioned Officers.

The history of those from Athol will be found under their respective names.

1st Lieut. Benj. H. Brown was left sick at Algiers La. April 9, 1863; rejoined the Company May 13th. Was sick at the capture of Port Hudson.

2d Lieut. V. V. Vaughan, was detailed in charge of Convalescent Camp, Carrolton La. Jan. 1863; returned to the Company May 2d, and returned to Mass. sick, after the fall of Port Hudson.

Sergeant A. T. King was sick after May, 1863.
1st Corporal Alonzo French was appointed

Corporal May 1, 1863 in the place of George O. Richardson, reduced to the ranks for absence.

Edward F. Stratton was sick from April 19, to May 15.

G. C. Warner was detailed Color Guard, Feb. 2d 1863.

E. E. Bissell was in Hospital from Feb. 10th till Aug. 11, 1863.

C. W. Kendall was detailed in Quarter Master's Department April 8, 1863, and Freeman G. Perry was made Corporal in his place.

Corporal G. W. Knights died in New Orleans April 10, 1863, and J. Orlando Gould was made Corporal in his place. Mr. Gould also died July 27, 1863.

Company E, of the 53d Regiment, remained in Camp with the Regiment at Carrolton La. from Feb. 1, 1863 till March 5, when it left for Baton Rouge and arrived there on the 7th of the same month. March 13, it marched with the forces of the Department on Port Hudson, but as the attack on the latter place was postponed it returned to Baton Rouge March 20th. April 1, it left for Algiers La. and arrived there the next day. April 9, it marched for Berwick Bay, and two days later started with the expedition under Gen. Banks for Opelousas and Alexandria La.

On the 12th and 13th of April, it was engaged in the battles of Fort Bisland, when the Regiment was for the first time under fire. The Fort was captured, and April 20, the Army reached Opelousas. The weather was very hot, and the roads very dry and dusty, but the men moved on like veterans. The whole distance marched when the Regiment had reached Opelousas was 480 miles. The Regiment left for Alexandria May 5, and arrived there on the 8th. On the 18th, it was at Simsport, 75 miles from Alexandria, and it crossed the Atchafalaya River on the 20th. May 22d at 7 o'clock P.M. it embarked on board the Laurel Hill for Bayou Sara, and arriving on the 23d, marched at once to join the Brigade in the rear of Port Hudson. The night following, the whole Regiment was on picket duty, and the next day it moved forward with the whole force. May 24th the Regiment skirmished in the woods as guard for the Engineer Corps, and led the column. On the evening of the next day, the Regiment relieved the 91st New York Reg. as advance picket, and about 9 o'clock P.M. received a volley from the enemy with some loss. The firing was returned, and at daylight, an attack on the left was repulsed. May 27th the Regiment moved forward in line of battle for the first general attack upon Port Hudson. At 7½ o'clock, it was ordered to the front to support the 1st Maine

Battery, when for two hours it was under a continuous fire of shot and shell. At 10½ o'clock, it was again ordered forward to the front line of skirmishers, where it engaged the sharp shooters of the enemy and held the point till the afternoon of the next day. Up to this time the loss in the Regiment had been thirty killed and wounded. From the last mentioned date, the Regiment was under fire, building breast-works and doing picket duty, for the space of eight days. June 5, it marched with the Brigade in pursuit of the enemy to Clinton La. but returned without an engagement after four days. The heat was now intense, and this expedition was unusually severe.

Having returned to Port Hudson, the Regiment early in the morning of June 14th advanced as third line of skirmishers in the second general attack upon Port Hudson. The battle continued all that day, with a loss in the Regiment of Eighty six killed and wounded. The sufferings of that day were terrible, for the assault proved a failure. After this the Regiment supported Battery A, U. S. Artillery till the surrender of Port Hudson. Since leaving Opelousas, the Regiment had marched 280 miles. The losses before Port Hudson in Company E were two killed and eight wounded.

Port Hudson was surrendered to Maj. Gen.

Banks July 8, 1863 and the next day the 53d Regiment left for Plain Stores. July 11th our men started for Baton Rouge, and on the 15th went to Donaldsonville La. where they remained till orders were received to prepare to leave for home. The detailed and sick men were brought together, and Aug. 12th the Regiment left Baton Rouge for the North by the way of the Mississippi River and Cairo Ill. From Cairo the journey was made by Rail Road to Fitchburg and the Regiment arrived at the latter place on the morning of Aug. 24th 1863. At Fitchburg a public reception was given to the Regiment by the people from the towns in which the several Companies had been recruited. Isaac Stevens Esqr was the member of the General Committee for Athol, and Calvin Kelton Esqr was appointed by the citizens of Athol their Marshal. With Messrs Stevens and Kelton were associated Mr. Dexter Aldrich, Mr A. L. Cheney, Dr A. G. Williams and Rev. John F. Norton as a Committee to assist in caring for the sick soldiers. Of these six were found who were at once brought home by their friends and by the Committee, viz. Daniel Casavant, Lauriston I. King, Charles H. Tyler, Charles V. Goddard, Warren E. Smith and Azro B. Folsom.

All the members of the Company were permitted to return home on the evening of the

9*

same day; and they were welcomed at the Athol
Depot by a large concourse of their friends and
fellow citizens.

Sept. 2d the men were discharged from the
service of the United States, their term of enlistment having expired; and Sept. 10th those
belonging to Company E, were paid off at the
Office of Capt. F. F. Fay.

Though they enlisted for nine months only,
nearly or quite an entire year was consumed by
these men in military service.

Of the 96 officers and soldiers constituting
Company E, 53d Regiment, who were mustered
into the United States service at Camp Stevens,
Groton Junction, Oct. 17, 1862, one, viz Spencer Stockwell of Athol died in said Camp. While
the Company was in Franklin Street Barracks,
New York City, Geo. B. Wood was discharged,
and died the next day.

B. H. Doane of Royalston being sick was also
discharged in New York before the Regiment
left for the seat of War, while Charles P. Bliss
of New Salem joined Company E, and was mustered into the service in New York. The number of men in the Company when it embarked
for New Orleans was therefore ninety four. Of
these Lauriston I. King of Athol and George H.
Wood of Royalston were left in the Hospital at
New York sick. Mr. King at a later period joined

his Company at the seat of War, but Mr. Wood was unable to do so.

Seventeen men of Company E, including Spencer Stockwell were either killed in battle or died of wounds or disease while these men were in service, viz.

Spencer Stockwell, Nov. 20, 1862, at Groton Junction, Diphtheria.

George L. Hancock, March 29, 1863, Carrolton La. C. Diarrhœa.

George W. Knights, April 10, 1863, New Orleans, of C. Diarrhœa.

Uri C. Day, April 18, 1863, Baton Bouge, of C. Diarrhœa.

W. J. Cleaveland, April 24, 1863, Berwick Bay, Measles.

Charles E. Tenney, April 26, 1863, New Orleans, C. Diarrhœa.

Henry C. Moore, April 29, 1863, New Orleans, C. Diarrhœa.

Henry S. Smith, May 9, 1863, Berwick Bay, Brain Fever.

John M. Wood, May 15, 1863, Baton Rogue, C. Diarrhœa.

Walter T. Putnam, June 14, 1863, Port Hudson, Killed in Battle.

Adin Oakes, June 29, 1863, Baton Rouge, Wounds.

C. H. Bliss, July 1, 1863, New Orleans, C. Diarrhœa.

Abner E. Towne, July 3, 1863, Baton Rogue, C. Diarrhœa.

Cyrus W. Conant, July 10, 1863, New Orleans, C. Diarrhœa.

Marshall Collins, July 14, 1863, Baton Rogue, C. Diarrhœa.

J. O. Gould, July 27, 1863, Baton Rogue, C. Diarrhœa.

E. L. Smith, July 29, 1863, New Orleans, C. Diarrhœa.

After the return of the Company, viz Nov. 2d, 1863, Lauriston I. King died of disease contracted in the service.

Of the ninety seven men including C. P. Bliss, composing Company E, three were discharged and seventeen died before the return of the Regiment, leaving seventy seven to be accounted for, which was the number mustered out of service at Camp Stevens, Groton Junction, Sept. 2d, 1863.

During the month of April 1863, the average number of men belonging to this Company who were fit for military duty was not far from 55. In May, it was reduced to 41 or 42. In June, it was not more than 32, while it was sometimes as low as 24. In July, it was about the same, and at the surrender of Port Hudson, the Company mustered but 25 non-commissioned Officers and Privates.

It is remarkable, not that so many of the men were sick but rather that any were well, when we consider that the men had not become acclimated, that their encampments were often in unhealthy locations, that the heat was very oppressive, that their marches were long and tedious and their service in the trenches before Port Hudson exceedingly exhausting.

The pledge that follows throws light upon the moral condition of this Company.

" We the undersigned, members of Capt. F. F. Fay's Company, realizing the necessity of guarding against the evil temptations that are liable to come in contact with young men just commencing the duties of a soldier's life, and being desirous of returning to our homes at the expiration of nine months, with characters as pure and unsullied as when we bid our friends adieu ; Now therefore, do hereby pledge ourselves to abstain from the use of all intoxicating drinks as a beverage during the said period of nine months ; and moreover by our influence, both in *word* and in *deed* we pledge ourselves to discountenance every thing that tends to profanity, vulgarity or obscenity and at all times to conduct ourselves as pure, high minded men.

Camp Stevens, Groton Junction Oct. 2, 1862."

To this are attached the names of F. F. Fay Captain, B. H. Brown 1st Lieut., V. V. Vaughan 2d Lieut. and of other members of the Company to the number of Sixty Six.

Commissioned Officers.

Of these Athol furnished Fifteen.

George H. Hoyt was 2d Lieutenant and Captain in the 1st Kansas Cavalry, and at a later period Lieut. Colonel in the 15th Kansas Cavalry.

James Oliver Jr. was Assistant Surgeon and Surgeon of the 21st Regiment Mass. Volunteers, and Assistant Surgeon and Surgeon of the 61st

Regiment.   In June 1865 he was made Brigade Surgeon.

Alfred G. Williams was Assistant Surgeon in the 11th Regiment and at a later period Contract Surgeon on board the Hospital Boat " Nashville," on the Mississippi River and in the Hospital of the Rebel Prisoners at Elmira N. York.

Rev. John N. Mars was Chaplain of the 1st North Carolina Colored Regiment.

Farwell F. Fay was Captain of Company E, of the 53d Regiment and afterward Assistant Adjutant General of Mass. for recruiting purposes in the Department of Mississippi, assigned to the staff of Lieut. Colonel E. C. Kinsley.

Adin W. Caswell was for three years service Captain of Company B, 27th Regiment.

Ransom Ward was Captain of Company H, 1st Kansas Colored Infantry, now designated as 79th U. S. Infantry.

Daniel W. Larned of the 27th Regiment was made Captain in said Regiment under the Governor's order May 15, 1865.

George R. Hanson who had been in the Band of the 27th Reg. Inf. and in the 2d Heavy Artillery was commissioned 1st Lieutenant and afterwards Captain in the 14th U. S. Colored Heavy Artillery.

Albert D. Pond of the 27th Regiment was made 1st Lieutenant May 9, 1865.

John O. Mowry of the same Regiment, in 1863 was made 2d Lieutenant of Company I of the 55th (Colored) Regiment, and afterward 1st Lieutenant of Company B, and then Quartermaster of the same Regiment.

Lovell H. Horton was 2d Lieutenant of Company B, 27th Regiment.

Asa L. Kneeland was 2d Lieutenant of Company K and 1st Lieutenant of Company F of the 32d Regiment.

John D. Emerson of the 2d Regiment and afterwards a Sergeant in the Signal Corps was made 2d Lieutenant in the 2d New York Heavy Artillery, June 1865.

Seth F. Hale of the 21st Regiment was commissioned 2d Lieutenant in the Mass. Militia, May 1865.

The promotion of Non-Commissioned Officers, so far as this can be ascertained, will be noticed under the head of "Personal History" in this Record.

Of the families in Athol that made great sacrifices to suppress the rebellion many deserve an honorable notice in this Record.

James L. Merrill furnished five sons for the army, all of whom were courageous and faithful soldiers. Of these, three were very severely

wounded while the fourth nearly sacrificed his
life to save that of a wounded brother.

The family of Leander Phelps furnished four
to fill the quotas from Athol, two of whom re-
enlisted, and another entered the service a second time and was severely wounded.

Franklin Oliver had four sons in the service,
one of whom was severely wounded and another
died in the rebel prison at Andersonville Ga.

Isaac King had also four sons in the service,
two of whom are dead.

Albert Simonds followed two of his sons into
the ranks and one of the latter was a prisoner at
Andersonville and in other rebel prisons.

Laban Morse Esqr. was our agent for the relief of our sick and wounded at Newbern N.
C. and sent two sons to the war.

George Morse went himself as a soldier and
two of his sons did the same. '

Edward Nickerson had three sons in the army, one of whom was a prisoner at Andersonville and in other places.

Widow Dorinda Foster had three sons in the
army, one of whom died in the service and
another not long after his discharge.

William Hill went into the service with two
sons and was killed at Roanoke Island and one
son died at the same place.

Subscriptions to the Fund for paying Citizens' Bounties under the several calls for Troops, exclusive of the amounts paid in 1862. For the latter see page 50 of this Record.

One of the Subscription Books circulated in District No. 1, under the call July 18, 1864, it has been impossible to find, but the lack of it has been supplied as far as possible. About Twenty Five Dollars however were paid upon that subscription that will not appear upon the pages that follow.

The different subscriptions of each subscriber are embraced in a single sum. Entire correctness has been aimed at, in bringing together these amounts, but it is more than possible that some mistakes have been made.

Amsden, Washington H.	$95	Bruce, F.	35
Amsden, O.	10	Bangs, N.	41
Aldrich, D.	70	Bangs, A.	51
Allen F.	66	Bacon, J. B.	5
Adams, H. B.	79	Beard, R.	65
Adams, C. H.	28	Burbeck, J. W.	55
Adams, B.	5	Babbitt, M. F.	11¼
Ames, Miss Alpha	2	Babbitt, T.	5
Black, G. W.	75	Babbitt, L. D.	53
Baker, M.	50	Babbitt, G. W.	25
Batchelder, L.	6	Bullard, D.	36
Bailey, I.	46	Bullard, J. H.	15
Boutelle, J.	16	Bullard, B. F.	90
Blake, T. H.	8	Bullard, F.	15
Bruce, A. C.	26	Benjamin, F. J.	46

Bassett, C. C.	75	Clark, J. E.	42
Bassett, C. C. Mrs.	10	Casavant, D.	15
Bassett, E.	3	Casavant, J.	17
Brown, O. B.	5	Croney, F. A.	25
Brown, W. C.	5	Oardany, J. B.	71
Brown, E. F.	45	Collier, J.	25
Bemis, S. A.	10	Coolidge, J.	57
Ball, J. A.	30	Coolidge, H. R.	5
Bates, F.	10⅘	Conant, A. B.	35
Bottomly, F.	5	Conant, A. W.	5
Bannam, G.	⅜	Cheney, A.	15
Brooks, O. T.	51	Cheney, D.	30
Bancroft, C. O.	26	Clapp, S.	21⅘
Brock, N. H.	23	Clapp, E. P.	5.
Ballard, F. D.	13	Carpenter, C. F.	25
Bigelow, D.	12	Cunningham, B.	5
Bigelow, O. J.	30	Collar, L. S.	40
Briggs, M.	20	Collar, G.	5
Briggs, J. S.	5	Collar, C. W.	16
Briggs, T. M.	25	Crossman, M.	5
Briggs, W.	26	Cummings, S.	⅜
Briggs, S. B.	10⅔	Davenport, C. W.	81
Bryant, ——.	20	Davenport, J.	10
Boler, J.	4	Davenport, O. P.	32
Bliss, S. W.	3	Davenport, D. B.	11
Bannon, C. W.	71	Davenport, Mrs. L.	10
Barber, H. R.	66	Davis, K.	3
Barnes, C. J.	25	Davis, J. H.	26
Belden, J. H.	30	Drake, B. B.	3
Barry, G.	10	Doyle, T.	1
Chubb, A. S.	35	Dunbar, J. F.	25
Carter, A. W.	63	Dexter, J. L.	12
Chase, A. P.	8	Drury, D.	56
Chase, S. D.	5	Drury, H.	15
Chase, E. F.	41	Drury, E.	30

Drury, E. A.	80	Folsom, A. B.	30
Drury, W.	23	Goddard, G.	50
Drury, J. R.	95	Goddard, F.	56
Drury, G. W., Jr.	10	Goddard, D.	15
Drury, Jona, 2d	40	Goddard, David	25
Drury, J.	13	Goddard, A.	28
Drury, S. S.	15	Gage, D.	5
Drury, G. W., 2d	15	Gage, E.	25
Ellis, E.	95	Gage, M.	15
Elmore, S.	3	Gage, E. J.	18
Eaton, O.	24	Gage, H. H.	23
Fuller, J. E.	50	Gage, S.	6
Fuller, F.	35	Goodspeed, T. H.	85
Fay, F. F.	75½	Garfield, R.	20
Fay, F. R.	15	Garfield, G. R.	18
Fay, J. H.	40	Glennon, J.	7
Fay, W. G.	15	Gardner, J.	14½
Fay, S. E.	71	Gray, H.	10
Fay, L. B.	51	Gray, W. N.	30
Fish, S.	110	George, F. T.	10
Fish, W. W.	90	Gerry, G. M.	15
Fish, W.	15	Gibbs, W. L.	3
Fisher, C. D.	30	Hanson, J. N.	60
Friends	22	Holton, J. A.	50
Fletcher, A. F.	60	Holton, S.	5
Fletcher, A. V.	46	Hapgood, L. W.	44
Farr, H.	8	Hathaway, S. B.	5
Farr, G.	74	Horton, L. H.	45
Frost, W. H.	5	Horton, E. B.	22
Flint, J.	3	Hill, A.	24
Flint, C. F.	10	Hill, M.	133
Fry, J.	35	Hill, J. C.	30
Foskett, W.	33	Harding, A. Jr.	30
Field, C.	34	Haven, J.	55
Foster, N.	5	Haven, J. F.	23

Lord, E.............	70	Perry, J. W..........	65
Lord. A.............	12	Peck, W.............	25
Lord, F. G. & Co.....	15	Peck, P. L...........	10
Lord, N. Y...........	90	Pond, G. S.	50
Lewis, J. S..........	6	Pond, F. L...........	18
Lewis, J..	16	Pratt, A............	4
Lewis E. T..........	10	Pitts, S. W..........	20
Lewis, J. L..........	10	Pitts, S. B..........	66
Lewis, H. A..........	15	Prouty, A...........	$6\frac{3}{4}$
Lord, Emerson........	5	Prouty, S. D.........	5
Lord, J.............	7	Prouty, G...........	5
Morse, C. B..........	41	Putnam, R...........	56
Morse, C. W.........	56	Puffer, E. A.........	5
Morse, S. R..........	15	Packard, J. F........	8
Moore, S.	23	Rickey, G. W........	60
Moore, A............	10	Rich, F.............	36
Moore, C. W.........	15	Richardson, N........	75
Merriam, O.	65	Richardson, C. F.....	45
McLane, N...........	10	Richardson, G. H.....	51
Miller, I............	$5\frac{1}{5}$	Reynolds, C. W.......	5
Mann, W............	60	Rice, J. M..........	80
Meachum, J. C.......	28	Rice, C. E..........	10
McRay, G.	5	Rice, S. R..........	$\frac{3}{20}$
Norton, J. F.........	16	Raymond, F. H.......	10
Nourse, H. C.	48	Reynolds, H. L.......	23
Nelson, G. W........	10	Shaw, F. W..........	25
Newton, W	20	Smith, Erastus.......	39
Newton, S...........	4	Smith, Royal........	10
Newell, A...........	20	Smith, D.	66
Olds, W.............	$2\frac{3}{8}$	Smith, David........	55
Oliver, Ozi	45	Smith, H. C.........	44
Oliver, O............	5	Snith, E...........	20
Parmenter, F. C......	60	Smith, W...........	10
Parmenter, J. S.......	115	Smith, A...........	10
Perry, F. G..........	40	Smith, R...........	15

10*

Smith, J. W	26	Sprague, G	10
Smith, W	5	Sprague, L. K	56
Shepherd, Joseph	10	Sprague, F. M	38
Shepherd, J	4	Sanborn, W. B	15
Southard, G	65	Sloan, J. W	11⅜
Sawyer, A. M	65	Sibley, S	3
Sawyer, J. W	55	Thorpe, W	115
Sawtelle, J. F	30	Thorpe, F	38
Stockwell, J	5	Thorpe, O	10
Stockwell, C	25	Thorpe, A	10
Stockwell, S. J	46	Thorpe, L	15
Stockwell, S	20	Tolman, A	15
Stockwell, O. J	15	Tolman, C. F	10
Snow, J. W	18	Tolman, J. C	3
Southland, H. H	10	Thrower, W. L	5
Spear, C. T	6	Tenney, G. L	20
Scott, O. A	40	Thomas, E. A	46
Stratton, A. G	79	Thomas, A. M	5
Stratton, A. T	33	Thomas, G	5
Stratton, J. H	11⅛	Taylor, E. M	10
Stratton, J	18	Tyler, P. C	35
Stratton, Joseph	26	Tyler, C. H	15
Stratton, A. O	5	Totman, J. F	14
Stratton, R	40	Townsend, R. F	35
Stratton, G. L	85	Townsend, A	8
Sanderson, C	5	Townsend, J	25
Simonds, L. B	15	Townsend, H. P	10
Simonds, N	5	Townsend, C. A	75
Stevens, I	29	Townsend, H. D	15
Spooner, C. M	105	Twichell, S. F	40
Stone, D. H	20	Twichell, B. M	15
Stone, J. W	3	Twichell, E. L	20
Swan, O	5	Twichell, E. C	43
Swan, J	74	Utley, G. D	65
Savage, T. W	15	Utley, Mrs	10

Underwood, G. P.	25	Ward, L.	5
Underwood, C.	20	Ward, N.	10
Williams, J. H.	80	Wiggins, W. S.	28
Williams, E.	5	Wiley, I. L.	10
Wood, J. C.	58	Wiley, N.	15
Wood, J. E.	26⅜	Walker, F. H.	20
Wood, C. C.	22	Willard, E. A.	50
Wood, B. E.	25	Waite, A. J.	50
Wood, Joseph E.	5	Wheeler, J.	5
Wood, D. F.	65	Wheeler, J. A.	5
Wood, G.	21⅜	Willey, G. W.	26
Wood, J. K.	5	Willey, A.	3
Worcester, G. H.	15	Woodard, G. W.	38
Woodis, J. C.	5	Woodard, C. W.	16
Whitney, J. W.	3	Young, E. S.	25
Whitney, J. P.	28	Amount	$12,588
Whitney, G. H.	54	Not included in the	
White, J.	10	above	25
Warren, G. H.	10		
Wilder, G.	60		$12,613
Ward, D. A.	25		

Of this sum there was refunded to the subscribers to raise funds under the last call for troops, unexpended money to the amount of $997, leaving as actually expended by the citizens of Athol to fill the different quotas in 1864 $11,616.

The Towns and cities of the Commonwealth having been authorized to raise by taxation or otherwise funds "to reimburse money paid for recruiting purposes," by the individual citizens of any Town or City in the year 1864,

At a Town meeting legally called for June 10, 1865, it was

"Voted that the Town of Athol pay the several amounts contributed by individuals towards filling the several quotas of the Town or furnishing men for the service of the United States, under the several calls of the President of the United States or of the War Department, during the year 1864; and that the same shall be ascertained by the Selectmen and paid under their direction, the payment to be made on and after the 15th day of October next; and the sum of Thirteen Thousand Dollars or so much thereof as shall be necessary be raised and appropriated for that purpose. And no payment shall be made unless the claim is presented and proved, before Sept. 1, 1865."

"Voted that so much money as shall be necessary to make the payments named in the foregoing vote, not exceeding Thirteen Thousand Dollars, be raised and assessed as a special tax, the bills to be committed on or before the 15th day of Sept. next, and the tax collected and paid into the treasury on or before the 15th day of October next."

"Voted that no discount shall be allowed on this tax, and certificates of the Selectmen of the amount of money contributed by individuals for said purposes shall be accepted by the Collector in payment of the Tax."

At a Town Meeting, Aug. 16, 1865 the votes above recorded that were passed on the 10th day of June 1865, were rescinded, and by a vote of 141 in the affirmative and 98 in the negative, it was

"Voted that it is not expedient for the Town to raise funds to refund the money contributed by individuals for recruiting purposes in the year 1864."

And at another Town Meeting Aug. 28, 1865, a vote in precisely the same language was passed by 257 in the affirmative and 100 in the negative.

The record of what the people of Athol have done to aid in suppressing the Great Rebellion will be incomplete unless some statements are made respecting the hospital stores and supplies of various kinds that were furnished for the relief and comfort of our brave and patriotic soldiers. During the whole period covered by this record, individuals, families and neighborhoods were sending money and boxes of food and clothing to their kindred and friends in the army. No attempt will be made to estimate the value of these supplies, but we may safely say that they were deemed by the recipients of them invaluable.

To the Christian Commission and one or two other agencies engaged in relieving our sick and wounded soldiers money was forwarded to the amount of $350.00. Soon after the war commenced the Ladies organized a Soldiers Aid Society in each of the two large villages, and these were in active operation till peace was restored. Of the Society in the Centre of the Town Mrs. Dr. George Hoyt was President and Mrs. Thomas H. Goodspeed Secretary and Treasurer, and this furnished supplies as follows.

May 4, 1861, a Box of Hospital supplies valued at	$33.85
May 27, 1861, a Box of Hospital supplies.......	260.00
Oct. 4, 1861, Soldiers' Comforts.............	75.00
Oct. 16, 1861, Box of Quilts, Sheets &c........	249.50
Sept. 6, 1862, 2 barrels Clothing &c.	127.00
Dec. 22, 1862, 1 barrel dried Apples	9.37
Jan. 8, 1863, Box of Clothing	55.00
May 8, 1863, Barrel dried Apples............	10.00
July 11, 1863, Barrel dried Apples............	12.25
Jan. 3, 1864, 3 barrels Clothing &c...........	100.00
June 1, 1864, 1 Box of Cotton and Linen	25.00
Sept. 27, 1864, 5 Barrels of Vegetables, 1 Barrel Clothing....................	75.00
March 14, 1865, 2 barrels of Clothing	90.00
June 30, 1865, 1 barrel of Clothing ...:........	45.00
June 30, 1865, Cash sent to Sanitary Commission..	28.50
Knitting 80 pairs of socks........	28.00

Total amount of supplies forwarded chiefly by Mrs. Goodspeed.................... $1223.47

The Soldiers Aid Society in Athol Depot of which Mrs. Walter Thorpe was the President till May 12, 1864 when Mrs. Otis Bancroft was appointed upon Mrs. Thorpe's resignation, was in operation from the beginning till the end of the war.

Miss Ellen M. Bigelow, Mrs. S. E. Fay, Miss Nettie Hill, Mrs. Harding R. Barber and Mrs. Lucius Sprague filled successively the office of Secretary and Treasurer of this Society; while its first President Mrs. Walter Thorpe was appointed Assistant Manager of the Sanitary Commission in 1865. This Society sent through the Sanitary Commission for the relief of our soldiers eleven Boxes and three Barrels chiefly of Hospital stores and supplies, the total value of which was estimated to be $808.43.

Through what may be called the public channels of aid to the soldiers, Athol therefore furnished, in money and supplies to the amount of $2381.90. Add to this, Hospital stores sent in 1862 directly to Dr. Otis, Surgeon of the 27th Regiment at Newbern of the value of ninety five dollars and we have the sum of $2470.90 all of which was cheerfully given to comfort and succor the brave defenders of our country.

The total amount of indebtedness incurred by the Town of Athol on account of the war is ascertained by the Selectmen to be $18,880.94.

Of which there has been paid $8,987.36.

Leaving unpaid March 1865 $9,893.58.

Individual citizens have contributed to pay bounties $12,777.78.

The cost of Substitutes and the amount paid for Commutation under the draft in 1863 was about $5430, making the total amount of expenses $39,565.62.

No reference is here made to the large sums contributed for the comfort of the soldiers in a less public manner.

EXPLANATION OF THE TABLES THAT FOLLOW.

1. No distinction is made in these Tables between Non-Commissioned Officers and Privates, as it seems desirable to give the names of the soldiers Alphabetically.

2. The Age of each is that given at the time of enlistment.

3. Blanks in the columns of Bounties indicate that no bounties were paid by the Town or by the citizens of Athol. No attempt is made to indicate the bounties paid by the State or by the United States.

4. Blanks elsewhere indicate simply a failure to obtain the desired information.

5. As a general rule, the soldiers whose age, birthplace, occupation &c., are not given, were obtained through Brokers.

6. In the case of the 53d Regiment the exact sum named was paid to each soldier as a Private or Citizens' bounty. In all other cases, this Column indicates only the *average* sum paid by the citizens in procuring the several recruits under a particular call for troops. To fill the same quota some received more than others, but the average amount is the only matter of any considerable consequence.

11

ATHOL MEN IN THEIR REGIMENTS, COMPANIES, ETC.

Second Regiment.

NAME.	Comp'y.	Where Born.	Age.	Occupation.	Married or Sin.	Town Bounty.	Cit'n's Bounty.
J. R. Billings	F	Troy, N. H.	32	Shoemaker.	Single.		
David F. Billings	F	Concord, N. H.	28	"	"		
John Buckley							
William L. Clutterbuck	F	England.	24	Shoemaker.	Married.	$125.00	$51.50
Frederic Cummings	B	Athol.	20	"	"		
John Conley						125.00	236.13
James Conners						125.00	236.13
John D. Emerson	F	Royalston.	17	Student.	Single.		
Columbus Fox	F	New York.	33	Shoemaker.	"		
Aurin B. French	F	Winches'r, N. H.	22	Mechanic.	Married.		
Charles S. Green	F	Oakham.	20		Single.		
John Grawad						125.00	236.13
Charles H. Hill	I	Athol.	20	Shoemaker.	Single.		
Horace Hunt	F	Prescott.	28	Teacher.	"		
Thomas Johnson	B	Liverpool, Eng.	20	Operator.	"		
Charles Johnson						125.00	51.50
Lewis Johnson						125.00	51.50
Daniel Kelley						125.00	51.50
John King						125.00	236.13
Thomas McCarty						125.00	51.50
Edward McLaughlin						125.00	236.13
William Nute	F		25	Shoemaker.	Single.		

Name	Co.	Residence	Age	Occupation		Amount
Leander W. Phelps	F	Walpole, N. H.	31	Shoemaker.	Single.	
Delavan Richardson	F	Athol.	21	Machinist.	"	
Hubbard V. Smith	F	Shutesbury.	21	Mechanic.	"	125.00
Thomas Smith						236.13
Edward L. Townsend	F	Athol.	21	Painter.	Single.	

Fifth Regiment,
FOR 100 DAYS SERVICE.

Name	Co.	Residence	Age	Occupation	
George W. Lincoln	A	Leverett.	21	Mechanic.	Single.
George L. Tenney	A				
William I. Turner	A	Lunenburg.	18	Wheelwrig't.	Single.

Ninth Regiment.

Name	Co.	Residence	Age	Occupation	
Patrick Dempsey	K	Ireland.	28	Mechanic.	Married.
Warren A. Beaman	I	Millbury.	24	Shoemaker.	"

Tenth Regiment.

Name	Co.	Residence	Age	Occupation	
John F. Merrill	H	Greenfield.	21	Stone Mas'n.	Single.
James L. Merrill	H	Montague.	19	"	"

Eleventh Regiment.

Name	Co.	Residence	Age	Occupation	
A. G. Williams, As't Surg.		Stonington, Ct.	38	Apothecary.	Married.
Vernon S. Cook	B	Athol.	20	Shoemaker.	Single.

NAME.	Comp'y.	Where Born.	Age.	Occupation.	Mar'ied or Sin.	Town Bounty.	Cit'n's Bounty.
Twelfth Regiment.							
John W. Sprague......	1	Phippsburg, Me.	24	Plice Offic'r.	Married.	......	......
Thirteenth Regim'nt.							
Alfred Johnson......	C	Westminster.	20	Laborer.	Single.	......	......
Fifteenth Regiment.							
Maxon R. Wetherly......	R	Hardwick.	27	Mechanic.	Married.	......	......
Sixteenth Regiment.							
Daniel D. Bruce......	A	Petersham.	27	Shoemaker.	Single.	......	......
Guilford W. Lamb......	A	New Salem.	......	Mechanic.	"	......	......
Twentieth Regiment.							
John Brunt.	......	......	33	......	......	$125.00	$51.50
William Huffman......	......	......	33	......	......	125.00	51.50
Twenty-first Reg't.							
Jeduthan W. Ames......	A	Newport, N. H.	23	Mechanic.	Single.	125.00	51.50

Name	Co.	Residence	Age	Occupation	Condition		
Lewis P. Atwood	I	Warwick.	27	Farmer.	Married.		
Branch F. Ayers	A	Brandon, Vt.	18	Shoemaker.	Single.		
Cheney Boyd	K	Spencer.	31	"	"		
George Carter	A	Antioch, N. S.	28	Currier.	Married.		
Joseph H. Collins	A	Marlboro'.	21	Shoemaker.	Single.		
Collins W. Chittenden	A	Springfield, Vt.	23	Tinman.	Married.		
Joel B. Cummings	A	Athol.	34	Shoemaker.	Single.		
Patrick W. Fox	C	Meath, Ire.	18	Mechanic.	"		
Charles E. Hager	A	Athol.	18	Blacksmith.	"		
Seth F. Hale	A	Dana.	19	Shoemaker.	Married.		
Samuel A. Hill	A	Ches'rfi'ld, N. H.	25	"	Single.		
Andrew J. Hill	A	Athol.	18	Currier.	"		
William H. Johnson	A	"	30	Shoemaker.	"		
Owen Kenney	A	Manches'r, Eng.	20	Operator.	Married.		
Patrick Leonard	C	Ireland.	19	Shoemaker.	Single.		
Ansel Orcott	A	Montague.	26	Carpenter.	"		
James C. Parker	A	Stickney, C. E.	35	Mechanic.	Married.		
Charles C. Phelps	A	Athol.	23	"	Single.		
John E. Rand	A	St. Albans, Me.	20		"		
Levi F. Ripley	A	Tinmouth, Vt.	43		Married.		
George R. Severance	A	Orange.	18	Teamster.	Single.		
William A. Shepardson	A	Franklin.	18		"		
Charles E. Taft	K	Fitzwil'm, N. H.	18	Carpenter.	"	125.00	51.50
Morgan Young	...	...	44	Shoemaker.	Married.		
Jonathan D. Ward	A	Orange.	21	Mechanic.	Single.		
James Oliver, Jr., Surg'n	...	Athol.	27	Sur. & Phy'n.	"		

11*

NAME.	Comp'y.	Where Born.	Age.	Occupation.	Mar'ied or Sin.	Town Bounty.	Cit'n's Bounty.
Twenty-fourth Reg't.							
Edmund R. West........	A	......	......	Farmer.	......	......	......
Twenty-fifth Reg't.							
Francis B. Brock........	A	Dudley.	28	Shoemaker.	Single.	......	......
Henry D. Brock........	A	Athol.	19	"	"	......	......
William Cobb........						$125.00	......
Azor S. Davis........	E	Kingston, R. I.	32	Shoemaker.	Married.	100.00	......
Theodore J. Dyer......	I	Athol.	39	Laborer.	"	......	......
Albert Haskins........	I					......	......
Twenty-sev'th Reg't.							
Adin W. Caswell, Capt...	B	Wendell.	32	Mechanic.	Single.	......	......
Lovell H. Horton, 2d Lt.	B	Athol.	38	"	"	......	......
Andrew J. Ames........	K	Brattleboro', Vt.	18	Farmer.	"	......	......
Thomas G. Barry........	B	Leominster.	33	Mechanic.	"	......	......
Harry R. Blackmer......	B	Dana.	18	"		......	......
Joseph Bracewell......	B	England.	24	Operator.	Married.	100.00	......
John S. Briggs........	B	Athol.	37	Mechanic.	"	100.00	......
Lyman A. Chamberlain...	B	Dana.	22	Ostler.	Single.	......	......
John Clark........	B	Ireland.	34	Farmer.	Married.	......	......
Linus Crawford......	B	Pelham.	48	Shoemaker.	Single.	......	......

Name	Co.	Residence	Age	Occupation	Condition	Bounty
Henry N. Darling	B	England	27	Painter	Married	100.00
George S. Dresser	B	Orange	18	Farmer	Single	
George A. Flagg	C					125.00
Van Buren French	B	Athol	21	Shoemaker	Single	
Charles Gray	B	"	20	Mechanic	"	
William Hill	B	"	43	"	"	
James S. Hodge	B		44	"	Married	
John W. Howe	B	Richmond, N.H.	34	"	"	
Milton N. Jillson	B	Roxbury	23	"	"	
James Kelley	B	Athol	20	Miller	Single	
George L. Kendall	B	Roxbury	26	Mechanic	"	100.00
Daniel W. Larned	B	Orange	24	Sal'n Keep'r	"	
Fernaldo L. Lord	B	Athol	28	Painter	Married	100.00
Horatio W. McClellan	B	"	18	Farmer	Single	100.00
George W. Meacham	B	Petersham	36	Mechanic	Married	
Norris B. Meacham	B	Pelham	20	Farmer	"	
John O. Mowry	B	Athol	27	"	Single	
Edmund Moore	B	"	26	Mechanic	Married	
George Morse	B	"	44	"	Single	
John R. Morse	B	"	18	Shoemaker	"	
Otis Oliver	B		23	Mechanic	"	
Sylvanus E. Oliver	B	Royalston	26	Farmer	Married	
James Oliver 2d	B	Athol	28	Machinist	"	100.00
Aaron Oliver	B	"				
Franklin Oliver, Jr.	B	New Salem	21	Mechanic	Single	
J. Henry Packard	B		25	"	"	
Emory A. Peckham	B		18	"	"	

27th Regiment, Con.

NAME.	Comp'y.	Where Born.	Age.	Occupation.	Mar'ied or Sin.	Town Bounty.	City's Bounty.
Albert D. Pond	B	Holliston.	21	Mechanic.	Single.		
Foster W. Phelps	B	Dummerston, Vt.	24	"	"		
Samuel Rich	B	Athol.	25	"	"		
James H. Richardson	B		37	"	Married.		
Harvey Robbins	B	Warwick.	42	Turner.	"	$100,00	
Charles Sears	B	Barre.	35	Shoemaker.	"	100,00	
Albert Simonds	B	Winchendon.	43	Farmer.	"	100,00	
Joseph C. Smith	B	Athol.	27	Mechanic.	Single.		
Henry Smith	B	Canada.	24	Farmer.	"	100,00	
Lauriston A. Thorpe	B	Athol.	21	Mechanic.	"		
Robert W. Thrower	B	"	20	"	"		
George D. Townsend	B	"	21	"	"		
Nathaniel B. Twichell	B	Erving.	33	"	Married.	100,00	
Theodore Washburn	B				Single.		
Oscar Washburn	B	Athol.	15	Mechanic.	"		
E. Whipple Whitney	B	"	43	"	Married.	100,00	
Nelson G. Wool	B	Royalston.	22	Painter.	Single.	100,00	
Joseph F. Fay	Band	Athol.	30	Mechanic.	"		
George R. Hanson	"	New Salem.	19	"	"		
Thomas Kenney	"				"		
Henry T. Morse	"	Athol.	21	Wood Turn.	"		
Leander B. Morse	"	"	19		"		
William Richardson	"	Saugus.	37	Shoemaker.	Married.		

Name	Co.	Residence	Age	Occupation	Condition		
Twenty-eighth Reg't.							
John Buckley			26			125.00	$51.50
John Chartier						125.00	51.50
John Jones						125.00	51.50
John Madden			27			125.00	51.50
Thirtieth Regiment.							
William Bearl	E	Ireland	21	Operator	Single		
Sumner S. Giles	E	New Salem	19	"	"		
Asa Phillips	E	Hubbardston	30	Farmer	Married		
John Plunkett	E	Ireland	20	Operator	"	125.00	51.50
Charles Tilden	E		27	Farmer			
Chandler Whitney	E	Royalston	58	"	Married		
Thomas A. Woodward	E	England		Mason.	"		
Thirty-first Reg't.							
James A. Hand	H	Schenec'y, N. Y.	56	Mechanic	Married		
James Harkins		Ireland	23	Peddler	Single		
Patrick Reardon	B					125.00	Dis. Sep. '65.
Thirty-second Reg't.							
Jeduthan W. Ames	F	Newport, N. H.	21	Student	Single		

32d Regiment, Con.

NAME.	Comp'y.	Where Born.	Age.	Occupation.	Mar'ied or Sin.	Town Bounty.	Cit'n's Bounty.
Charles H. Barton	A	Athol.	19	Farmer.	Single.		
Eli Bodet	A	Masteros'a, C. E.	32	Carpenter.	Married.		
John M. Casavant	B	Westford, Vt.	21	Farmer.	"		
Frederic A. Chubb	B	Phillipston.	17	Student.	Single.		
George H. Clark	F	Athol.	16	Painter.	"		
James Connell	A	Ireland.	19	Farmer.	"		
Elmer G. Foster	B	Templeton.	20	Mechanic.	"		
William A. Fry	A	Salem.	34	Shoemaker.	Married.		
Gardner Howe	A	Marlboro'.	33	Mechanic.	"		
C. Dwight Kelton	F	Athol.	18	Farmer.	Single.		
Asa L. Kneeland	A	"	19	"	"		
Ebenezer Kneeland	F	"	17	"	"		
C. Walter Knowlton	F	"	17	Student.	"		
George W. Nelson	B	Richmond.	30	Currier.	Married.		
Henry D. Townsend	F	Athol.	19	Farmer.	Single.		
Horace K. Weaver	A	Orange.	24	"	Married.		

Thirty-fourth Reg't.

NAME.	Comp'y.	Where Born.	Age.	Occupation.	Mar'ied or Sin.	Town Bounty.	Cit'n's Bounty.
Otis E. Davis	E	Townsend.	34	Shoemaker.	Married.		
Walter R. Brown	E	Winchendon.	22	Mechanic.	Single.	100.00	
Joseph W. Howard	A	Northfield.	20	Farmer.	"	$100.00	$51.50

Thirty-sixth Reg't.

Name	Co.	Age	Occupation		Residence		
Warren E. Chamberlain	H	23	Shoemaker.	Married.	Petersham.	100.00	
John Doyle	D	45	Farmer.	"	Ireland.	100.00	
Charles D. Fisher	H	26	Shoemaker.	"	Templeton.	100.00	
Daniel W. Foster	D	28	Carpenter.	"	Phillipston.	100.00	
Martin L. Maynard	D		Blacksmith.		Winches'r, N.H.	100.00	
Joseph A. Merrill	H	19	Stone Mas'n.	Single.	Johnson, R.I.	100.00	
Henry S. Merrill	H	18	"	"	Providence, R.I.	100.00	
Jonathan B. Mills	D	34	Mechanic.	Married.	Warwick.	100.00	
Joshua Rich	H	32	"	"	Royalston.	100.00	
William J. Rogers	D	26	"	"	Wendell.	50.00	
Emory Sawin	D	44	Teamster.	"	Westminster.	100.00	
William Washburn	D	42	Carpenter.	"	Orange.	100.00	
Asa Wyman	K	43	Laborer.	"	Winchendon.	100.00	

Thirty-sev'nth Reg't.

Name	Co.	Age	Occupation		Residence		
William Donelly	I			Married.	Dis. June 21, '65.	125.00	236.13

Fifty-third Reg't.

Name	Co.	Age	Occupation		Residence		
Farwell F. Fay, Capt.	E	29	Lawyer.	Married.	New Salem.	100.00	
Adolphus Bangs	E	32	Clerk.	"	"	100.00	4.82
Harding R. Barber	E	23	Sal'n Keep'r.	"	Warwick.	100.00	4.82
Otis B. Boutwell	E	34	Mechanic.	"	Leverett.	100.00	4.82
Thomas Burns	E	35	Road Build'r.	"	Ireland.	100.00	20.00

53d Regiment, Con.

NAME.	Comp'y.	Where Born.	Age.	Occupation.	Married or Sin.	Town Bounty.	Gov'th's Bounty.
Daniel Casavant	E	Westford, Vt.	27	Leaf Dealer.	Single.	$100,00	$4,82
Ephraim F. Chase	E	Athol.	22	Clerk.	"	100,00	4,82
Edward P. Clapp	E	"	22	Painter.	"	100,00	4,82
Welcome J. Cleveland	E	Barre.	18	Shoemaker.	"	100,00	20,00
Marshall Collins	E	Marlboro'.	38	"	Married.	100,00	20,00
Cyrus W. Conant	E	Stowe.	25	Farmer.	Single.	100,00	4,82
Artemas W. Conant	E	"	23	"	"	100,00	4,82
Anthony V. Dimock	E	Chester, N. S.	28	Merchant.	Married.	100,00	4,82
George W. Drury, Jr	E	Athol.	29	Currier.	Married.	100,00	20,00
Simeon S. Drury	E	"	25	Tanner.	"	100,00	4,82
William G. Fay	E	"	40	Shoemaker.	"	100,00	4,82
Freeborn R. Fay	E	"	35	Ostler.	"	100,00	4,82
Levi B. Fay	E	Winches'r, N.H.	19	Barber.	Single.	100,00	4,82
Leyton W. Follett	E	Worcester, Vt.	24	Mechanic.	Married.	100,00	4,82
Azro B. Folsom	E	Winches'r, N.H.	32	Jeweller.	"	100,00	4,82
Byron A. French	E	Athol.	23	Mechanic.	"	100,00	20,00
Alfred Goddard	E	Royalston.	21	Farmer.	Single.	100,00	20,00
Charles V. Goddard	E	Athol.	18	"	"	100,00	4,82
J. Orlando Gould	E	"	28	"	"	100,00	20,00
Aaron H. Holt	E	South Hadley.	39	"	Married.	100,00	4,82
William A. Judd	E	"	24	Shoemaker.	"	100,00	20,00
Arthur N. Judd	E	"	18	"	Single.	100,00	4,82
Charles W. Kendall	E	Athol.	32	Har. Maker.	Married.	100,00	4,82
Lauriston I. King	E	"	28	Shoemaker.	"	100,00	10,00

Name	Co.	Residence	Age	Occupation	Condition		
Enoch T. Lewis	E	Royalston.	32	Mar'le Dea'r.	Married.	100.00	4.82
George W. Lincoln	E	Leverett. [C.F.	19	Mechanic.	Single.	100.00	4.82
George McRae	E	Williamstown,	28	"	Married.	100.00	20.00
James A. Moore	E	Athol.	22	Shoemaker.	Single.	100.00	20.00
George F. Moore	E	"	18	Teamster.	"	100.00	4.82
Adin Oakes	E	"	26	Sh'e P'g Mfr.	Married.	100.00	20.00
Ozi Oliver	E	"	28	Mechanic.	"	100.00	20.00
Freeman G. Perry	E	Harmony, Me.	27	"	Single.	100.00	20.00
John R. Pierce	E	Prescott.	43	"	Married.	100.00	4.82
Rufus Putnam	E	Leverett.	35	Painter.	"	100.00	4.82
Warren E. Smith	E	Hardwick.	27	Carpenter.	"	100.00	20.00
Henry H. Southland	E	Bellingham.	18	Ostler.	Single.	100.00	20.00
Peter Stanton	E	Ireland.	31	Farmer.	Married.	100.00	20.00
Harrison Stockwell	E	Athol.	22	Mechanic.	"	100.00	4.82
Spencer Stockwell	E	"	22	Farmer.	Single.	100.00	10.00
Henry H. Stratton	E	"	22	"	"	100.00	4.82
Frederic A. Stratton	E	"	18	Expressman.	"	100.00	4.81
William L. Thrower	E	Lancaster.	22	Farmer.	"	100.00	20.00
Harlan P. Townsend	E	Athol.	18	Student.	"	100.00	4.82
Charles H. Tyler	E	Hinsdale, N. H.	23	Clerk.	"	100.00	10.00
Freeman H. Walker	E	Athol.	25	Shoemaker.	Married.	100.00	10.00
David Walker	E	Scotland.	21	"	Single.	100.00	4.82
George B. Wood	E	Shutesbury.	20	"	"	100.00	20.00

55th Reg't. (Colored.)

Name	Co.	Residence	Age	Occupation	Condition		
John O. Mowry, 1st Lieut.	I	Pelham.	29	Farmer.	Married.		......

12

Fifty-sixth Reg't.

NAME.	Comp'y.	Where Born.	Age.	Occupation.	Married or Sin.	Town Bounty.	Cit'n's Bounty.
Leander B. Morse	I	Athol.	21	Wood Turn.	Single.		
Frederic P. Morse	G	"	21	Shoemaker.	"		
John E. Rand	E	St. Albans, Me.	22	Mechanic.	"		
William Richardson	G	Saugus.	39	Shoemaker.	Married.		
Frederic A. Stratton	B	Athol.	20	Expressman.	Single.		
Horace O. Thayer	B	Ware.	19	Laborer.	"		

Fifty-seventh Reg't.

NAME.	Comp'y.	Where Born.	Age.	Occupation.	Married or Sin.	Town Bounty.	Cit'n's Bounty.
John S. Brown	H	Lowell.	31	Farmer.	Married.		
Patrick W. Fox	H	Ireland.	21	Operator.	Single.		

1st Heavy Artillery.

NAME.	Comp'y.	Where Born.	Age.	Occupation.	Married or Sin.	Town Bounty.	Cit'n's Bounty.
Charles H. Barney		Cambridge.	33			$125.00	Dis. June '65.
George W. Meacham	C	Athol.	37	Carpenter.	Married.		
Chauncey Parkman, Jr	I	Northfield.	25	Mechanic.	Single.		
Leander W. Phelps	C	Walpole, N. H.	33	Shoemaker.	"		
Henry N. Smith	A		36	Mechanic.	Married.		
Florence Sullivan	C	Ireland.	26	Shoemaker.	Single.		

4th Heavy Artillery.

NAME.	Comp'y.	Where Born.	Age.	Occupation.	Married or Sin.	Town Bounty.	Cit'n's Bounty.
James Cotton	H	Ireland.	20	Laborer.	Married.	125.00	$236.13

Name	Co.	Residence	Age	Occupation	Condition		
Joseph E. Jennings	H	....	....	Farmer.	Single.	125.00	236.13
Peter Stanton	H	Ireland.	33	"	Married.	125.00	236.13
Clinton Teel	H	Wilmot, N. H.	18	"	Single.	125.00	236.13

11th U. S. Infantry.

Name	Co.	Residence	Age	Occupation	Condition		
Albert Horton	C	New Salem.	19	Shoemaker.	Single.		
John F. Nickerson	D	Chatham.	21	"	"		
Joseph Nickerson	D	"	19	"	"		
Ruel R. Nickerson	D	Cen. Falls, R. I.	16	"	"		
Charles A. Simonds	D	Athol.	19	Farmer.	"		
William O. Simonds	D	Winchendon.	17	"	"		
Willard Twichell	D	Athol.	38	"	Married.		

United States Navy.

Name	Co.	Residence	Age	Occupation	Condition		
John S. Clark		Detroit, Mich.	36	Farmer.	Married.		
Joseph F. Falvey		East Boston.	....	Seaman.	Single.	125.00	
John Humphrey		Athol.	23	Student.	"		
Elijah W. Lincoln		Leverett.	20	Mechanic.	"		
Lewis H. Sawin		Athol.	15	Student.			

Unassigned Soldiers.

Name	Co.	Residence	Age	Occupation	Condition		
Edgar Bent		Northfield.	18	Blacksmith.	Single.	100.00	
Silas Fry		Royalston.	52	Farmer.	Married.	100.00	
Charles H. Fry		Orange.	16	Shoemaker.	Single.	100.00	

Unassigned Soldiers.

NAME.	Comp'y.	Where Born.	Age	Occupation.	Mar'ied or Sin.	Town Bounty.	Cit'n's Bounty.
Zenas W. Lamb		Philipston.	23	Shoemaker.	Single.	100.00	
M. C. Mayo		Athol.	43	Carpenter.	Married.	100.00	
William McKee			16	Farmer.	Single.	100.00	
Joseph Miller		Athol.	19	Mechanic.	"	100.00	
Albert Miller		"	18	Farmer.	"	100.00	
George R. Phelps		"	19	Mechanic.	"	100.00	
Charles Streeter			24	Farmer.		100.00	
Benjamin M. Twichell, Jr.		Athol.	30	"	Married.	100.00	
William Twichell, Jr.		"	40	"	Married.	100.00	
Walter Wilber		New Salem.	26	Shoemaker.	Married.	100.00	

99th N. Y. Regiment, (COAST GUARD.)

NAME.	Comp'y.	Where Born.	Age	Occupation.	Mar'ied or Sin.	Town Bounty.	Cit'n's Bounty.
Amos H. Locke		Brattleboro', Vt.	24	Dag're Artist.	Single.	Musician.	
Charles L. Kendall		Athol.	22	Mechanic.	"	"	

2d Vermont Reg't.

NAME.	Comp'y.	Where Born.	Age	Occupation.	Mar'ied or Sin.	Town Bounty.	Cit'n's Bounty.
Joseph W. Kilburn	I	Warwick.	20	Shoemaker.	Single.		

NAME.	Where Born.	Age.	Occupation.	Mar'ied or Sin.
61st Mass. Infa'y.				
Isaiah S. Merrill...	Greenfield.	26	Stone Mas'n.	Single.
James Oliver, Jr...	Athol.	29	Surgeon.	"
3d Heavy Artill'y.				
George W. Stevens.	Fort Henry.	18	Mechanic.	Single.
7th Mass. Batte'y.				
Edwin C. Hastings.	Grantham.	24	Mechanic.	Married.
1st Col. N. Caro'a.				
John N. Mars.....	Norfolk, Ct.	58	Chaplain.	Married.
1st Kansas Cav'y.				
George H. Hoyt...	Athol.	....	Lawyer.	Single.
79th U. S. Inf. Col.				
Ransom Ward.....	Belchertown.	34	Merchant.	Married.
Sixth Battery.				
Peter Pelkey......	Burrillsville.	44	Laborer.	Married.
4th Conn. Reg't.				
G. W. Currier.......	....	....	....	....

NAME.	Where Born.	Age.	Town Bounty.	Cit'n's Bounty.
15th Reg't Infa'y.				
Robert O'Brian....	....	....	$125.00	$51.50
Abram Hodge.....	Prisoner.	....	125.00	51.50
19th Reg't Infa'y.				
Jeremiah Driscoll..	....	....	125.00	....
Julius Gerard.....	....	....	125.00	....
Robert McCarron..	....	....	125.00	....
William Smith....	Boston.	....	125.00	....

NAME.	Town Bounty.	Citiz'n's Bounty.	Remarks.
23d Reg't Infantry.			
Charles Smith........	$125.00	$236.13	....
26th Reg't Infantry.			
Terrence Donelly.....	125.00	51.50	Comp. I, Sin.
Charles Kent, Jr......	125.00	51.50	" A, "
33d Reg't Infantry.			
John L. Batchelder....	125.00	236.13	....
John Lynch.........	125.00	236.13	....
54th Reg't Infantry.			
Francis Powers.......	125.00	....	L'ves in Somers, Ct.
58th Reg't Infantry.			
John Lacy..........	125.00	....	Deserted March, '65.
3d Heavy Artillery.			
William Smith.......	125.00	51.50	....
William Hughes......	125.00	51.50	....
16th Heavy Artillery.			
Michael J. Hudson ...	125.00	236.13	Married.
Irving L. Leonard....	125.00	236.13	Single.
Peter Walters.......	125.00	236.13	....
1st Mass. Cavalry,			
Michael Broderick....	125.00	236.13	....
Michael Guilfoyle.....	125.00	....	Taunton, disch'd, June, '65.
3d Mass. Cavalry.			
Charles Fouquet......	125.00	236.13	....

NAME.	Town Bounty.	Citi'n's Bounty.	Remarks.
4th Mass. Cavalry.			
James Eagan.........	$125.00	Milton. Dis.	Nov. 14, 1865.
Irving C. Gates......	125.00	Hubbard'n, "	" " "
A. S. Ladd..........	125.00	....	....
W. F. Leavett........	125.00	....	....
J. E. Shattuck.......	125.00	Somerville,	Dis. Nov. '65.
Thomas Thompson....	125.00	Prov'nce, R. I.	" " "
5th Mass. Cavalry.			
John Bliss..........	125.00	236.13	One Year.
Nelson Jackson.......	125.00	236.13	Three Years.
George Michael......	125.00	236.13	Two "
Jacob Sadler........	125.00	....	....
Daniel T. Young......	125.00	236.13	....
Battalion Cavalry.			Frontier Ser.
George G. Clark......	125.00	....	One Year.
Peter A. Drollet......	125.00	....	One Year.
Edwin Holmes....	125.00	Discharged	June 30, 1865.
Willard Howard......	125.00	"	" " "
A. Keen............	125.00	"	" " "
1st Mass. Battery.			
Patrick T. Adams.....	125.00	51.50	....
Eleventh Battery.			
Joseph Hill.........	125.00	236.13	....
3d U. S. Infantry.			
William Hohenfels....	125.00	236.13	....
Henry Johnston......	125.00	236.13	....
Charles Wilson.......	125.00	236.13	....
5th Illinois Cavalry.			
John Mier..........	Representative Recruit for C. C. Bassett.		

19TH U. S. INFANTRY.   TOWN BOUNTY.   CITIZEN'S BOUNTY.

John Dorn,	$125.00.	$51.50.
Patrick Folly,	125.00.	51.50.
William Kennedy,	125.00.	51.50.
George Kennedy,	125.00.	51.50. ·
John Riely,	125.00.	51.50.

103D U. S. COLORED TROOPS, OBTAINED BY THE STATE.

Radley Fedley.   Credited to Athol.
Isaac Lucas.   "   "
Jacob Youngblood.   "   "

6TH COLORED HEAVY ARTILLERY.

Dennis Caldwell, Representative Recruit for Asa Hill.

1ST U. S. COLORED CAVALRY.

William Freeman, Representative Recruit for Walter Thorpe.

3D U. S. COLORED CAVALRY.

Daniel Bruce, Representative Recruit for Calvin Kelton.
Moses Wilkinson, Representative Recruit for Lewis Thorpe.
Henry Williams, Representative Recruit for D. F. Wood.

29TH MASS. UNATTACHED COMPANY.

Arthur N. Judd, $125.00 from Town, $236.13 from Citizens.

6TH MASS. CAVALRY.

James Harkins, see 31st Regiment.

FORTY-SECOND REGIMENT, (100 DAYS.)

Cutler Seaver, Company C; born in Milford, 17 years old, and a Mechanic.

SECOND HEAVY ARTILLERY.

George R. Hanson, see 27th Regiment.

Personal History of Athol Men while in the service of the United States for Suppressing the Great Rebellion.

Jeduthan W. Ames, 32d Reg. (See page 129) joined the First Battalion at Fort Warren in Feb. 1862. This Battalion as the 32d Reg. was ordered May 25, 1862 to take the field at the earliest possible moment, and Mr. Ames went with it to Washington and afterwards to Harrison's Landing on the James River Va. His health soon failed and after being sick three months he was discharged Nov. 22, 1862 and returned to Athol. Recovering his health he re-entered the service in the 21st Reg. early in the year 1864, joining the Reg. at Annapolis Md, Maj. Gen. Burnside being the Corps Commander; went with the Reg. into the great battles in Virginia and was wounded June 2, 1864 in the side, in the engagement at Bethesda Church. He was at once taken prisoner and removed to Richmond where he was kept three months, when he was exchanged, had a furlough, was in the Hospital two months and then discharged.

Andrew J. Ames, 27th Reg. (See page 126), went with the Reg. to Annapolis and under Gen. Burnside to the Coast of North Carolina early in the year 1862. During the long delay occasioned by storms and the difficulties encountered in crossing Hatteras Inlet, Mr. Ames suffered much, and his disease at length assumed the form of Congestion of the lungs which terminated fatally at Newbern N. C. April 2, 1862. He was buried at Newbern. His sickness prevented him from being in the ranks at the captures of Roanoke Island and Newbern.

Lewis P. Atwood, 21st Reg. (See page 125), went with the Reg. to Annapolis where he was sick with the Measles, but recovered sufficiently to join in the Expedition under Gen. Burnside to N. Carolina; was in the battle at the capture of Roanoke Island; was sick at the capture of Newbern; was in the battles at Camden N. C. the 2d Bull Run fight, Chantilly, Knoxville and Campbell's Station, Tennessee. Mr. Atwood was a nurse in the Hospitals at Boonsboro' and Frederick City Maryland 6 months; and reenlisting Jan. 1, 1864, he came home on a furlough of forty days; rejoined his Reg. at Annapolis in March 1864 and went with it to the front when Gen. Grant moved towards Richmond; was in the battle of the Wilderness and also at Spottsylvania, where he was severely wounded in the leg; was removed to Alexandria and June 1, was brought to the Hospital at Portsmouth

Grove R. I., where he remained in a very criti-
cal situation for a number of months when he
began to improve. Mr. A. was discharged as unfit for service March 10, 1865, and returned
home, lame, but recovering.

Branch F. Ayers, 21st Reg. (See page 125),
went with his Reg. to North Carolina and was
in the engagements at the Captures of Roanoke Island and Newbern; was sick of the Typhoid Fever and in the Hospital at Beaufort N.
C. and discharged as unfit for service June 30,
1862. In Sept. 1863, he reentered the service
returning to the same Reg. and was with the
Reg. in the battles at the Wilderness, Spottsylvania and on the North Anna, but his health
again failing he was discharged Oct. 8, 1864.

Adolphus Bangs, 53. Reg. (See page 131) went
with the Reg. to Louisiana, was in the battle at
the capture of Fort Bisland, and was sent from
that place to New Orleans, April 14, 1863, in
charge of the dead and wounded. Being sick,
Mr. Bangs entered the Marine Hospital at N. Orleans, May 7, 1863, where he remained till Aug.
11, 1863, when he rejoined his Reg. and returned
with it, Aug. 24, 1863. In the summer of 1864,
Mr. Bangs accompanied Capt. F. F. Fay to
Vicksburg and assisted him in recruiting from

the States in Rebellion for the State of Massachusetts.

Harding R. Barber, 53. Reg. (See page 131) went with the Reg. to Louisiana and was detailed in the Quartermaster's Department April 8, 1863. He rejoined his Company Aug. 9, 1863 and returned with it to his home Aug. 24, 1863 in good health.

Charles H. Barton, 32. Reg. (See page 130) was in the Battalion formed at Fort Warren in the Autumn of 1861, was very sick at the Fort, but gaining a little was brought home sick; recovering in part he returned to the Fort and went with the Battalion which had become the 32 Reg. to Washington and Harrison's Landing Va. Being sick, he was removed to the U. S. Hospital West Philadelphia, where after recovering he remained 14 months doing guard duty and being detailed for detective service, going often to Washington in charge of recruits and deserters. Reenlisting, he joined his Reg. and was with it when Gen. Grant moved towards Richmond; was sick with Fever and Ague three weeks in June 1864, was in the engagements when an advance was made upon the Weldon Rail Road, and at Hatcher's Run, went on the Weldon Rail Road raid during the following winter, was in the battles commencing March 28th 1865 which resulted in the capture of Richmond and the surrender of Gen. Lee's army, the 32d Reg. forming a part of the troops whose duty it was to receive the rebel arms; went to Farmville and Burkesville and then into camp when he was detailed for duty at Head Quarters being part of the time a mounted Orderly; was in the grand Review in Washington and finally was discharged with his Reg. June 29, 1865 and returned home in good health.

Thomas G. Barry, 27. Reg. (See page 126), went with the Reg. to N. Carolina and was in the engagement at the capture of Roanoke Island; while at that Island took a severe cold and was not able to participate in the capture of Newbern; remaining sick he was discharged Sept. 12, 1862 and returned to Athol where he died of the disease contracted in N. Carolina Oct. 18, 1862.

Warren A. Beaman, 9. Reg. (See page 123), was drafted July 1863 and reported for service, was mustered in Aug. 21, 1863 and joined the Reg. in Virginia. In May 1864 he was in the engagements when Gen. Grant moved towards Richmond and is supposed to have been taken prisoner in the battle of the Wilderness, or

about that time; was carried to Andersonville
Ga. and was in other rebel prisons; was sick of
Chronic Diarrhœa at the time when he was parolled for exchange at Charleston S. C. which
was in Dec. 1864; was brought to Annapolis
very low, and died there Jan. 2, 1865. His wife
went on to minister to him, but was delayed on
the way and he had been dead a few hours
when she reached the Hospital at Annapolis.
His remains were brought to Athol and buried
from the Church of the Evangelical Society,
Jan. 11, 1865. Mr. Beaman left in Athol a wife
and one child. At his request he had been
transferred to the 32d Reg. before his capture.

William Beard, 30. Reg. (See page 129),
went with his Reg. under Maj. Gen. Butler to Louisiana and participated in the movements that resulted in the capture of New Orleans. At a later
period he was with the Reg. in various engagements in Louisiana, and was in service at the
capture of Port Hudson. Early in 1864 Mr.
Beard reenlisted and came home on a furlough.
In July 1864 the Reg. was transferred to Virginia
and became a part of the Army of Gen. Sheridan
in the valley of the Shenandoah where the fighting was very severe — and at a later period participated in the great movements that resulted
in the defeat of Gen. Lee's army and the cap-

ture of Richmond. Mr. Beard is in service at this time, Jan. 1866.

Daniel F. Billings, 2d Reg. (See page 122), was among the first men that went from Athol into the service of the United States at the opening of the war, joining the Reg. at Camp Andrew, West Roxbury; went with the Reg. July 8, 1861 to the Upper Potomac, was in the engagements at Jackson Va. and afterwards in 1862 at Front Royal and Winchester during the advance of Gen. Banks up the Valley of the Shenandoah and his disastrous retreat. At a later period was in the engagements at Cedar Mountain, Antietam and Fredericksburg as well as in many other less known but desperate contests in Virginia, and in 1863 was in the battles at Chancellorsville and Gettysburg. In Aug. and Sept. 1863 Mr. Billings was with his Reg. in New York City for the suppression of riots and went with it to Tennessee to reinforce the army of Maj. Gen. Rosecrans. Reenlisting Jan. 1864, he came home on a furlough and rejoined his Reg. at Tullahoma Tenn. April 1864. Mr. Billings was taken sick and went into a Hospital at Murfreesboro' Tenn. where he remained after recovery, first, as cook, and then as Commissary. Meanwhile his Reg. under Gen. Sherman had penetrated Georgia and crossed the Carolinas, and he rejoined it in Alexandria Va. After the

Great Review at Washington, viz July 14, 1865 Mr. Billings was mustered out of the service and came home in good health, having served four years and two months.

J. B. Billings, 2d Reg. (See page 12), brother of the above, enlisting at the same time and going with his Reg. to Maryland and Virginia. But before the 2d Reg. participated in any noted engagements with the enemy, Mr Billings was taken sick, and being declared to be unfit for service he was discharged Feb. 17. 1862 and returned home feeble. His disease was Hernia; and from this he has gradually recovered, but has never been able to return to the service.

Harry R. Blackmer, 27. Reg. (See page 126), joined the Reg. in North Carolina with the first Company of recruits from Athol in the autumn of 1862; was in the engagements at Kinston, Whitehall, Goldsboro', Gum Swamp, and at the famous siege of Washington N. C. In Oct. 1863, he came with his Reg. to Newport News Va. and served with it in Norfolk and Portsmouth, having been promoted Corporal Aug. 14. 1863.

In Jan. 1864 Mr. Blackmer was attacked with the Small Pox, and died of this disease Jan. 28. at Norfolk Va. after a sickness of ten days. He was in the service about sixteen months, and during this time is said to have received 150 letters from his friends at the North all of which were answered.

Eli Bodet, 32. Reg. (See page 130), joined the Reg. in the Autumn of 1861 when it was the First Battalion at Fort Warren; went with the Reg. to Washington and to Harrison's Landing Va.; participated in the marches and trials of Porter's Corps in the retreat down the Peninsula and during the Campaign in Maryland, was with the Reg. supporting batteries at the battle of Antietam, was soon taken sick of Chronic Diarrhœa and removed to the Hospital at the Patent Office Washington, where he was found very low by Dr. J. P. Lynde of Athol who went to his relief; his discharge was obtained Jan. 22. 1863, and he was removed to New York on his way home where he died Jan. 26. 1863. Mr. Bodet's remains were brought on to Athol and buried from the church of the Evangelical Society, Jan. 29. 1863. He left in Athol a wife and two children.

Otis B. Boutwell, 53. Reg. (See page 131), went with his Reg. to Louisiana and Jan. 5. 1863 was detailed as 2d Bugler of the Regiment. Feb. 10. he was carried to the Marine Hospital N. Orleans sick with Rheumatic Fever, but recovering returned to his Company and to the ranks March 20. the vacancy occasioned by his sickness having been supplied. Mr. Boutwell was with the Regiment at the capture of Fort Bisland and on its march to Opelousas from which place he returned to the Hospital at New Orleans. Rejoined the Company June 20. 1863 and returned home with it Aug. 24. in comfortable health.

Cheney Boyd, 21. Reg. (See page 125), went with his Reg. into service in North Carolina; was in the engagement at the capture of Roanoke Island and Newbern; went with the Reg. in Aug. 1862 to Virginia and was in the 2d Bull Run battle and afterwards in the engagement at So. Mountain Maryland: was taken sick and after being in different Hospitals in Washington and Philadelphia, was discharged as unfit for service Jan. 1863, and returned to Athol.

Joseph Bracewell, 27. Reg. (See page 126), was among the recruits from Athol that joined the Reg. in N. Carolina in the autumn of 1862; was in the engagements at Kinston, Whitehall and Goldsboro'; was at Washington N. C. during its siege, was in the Conflict at Gum Swamp; went with his Reg. to Virginia and was taken Prisoner at Drury's Bluff Va. with most of his Reg. May 16. 1864; was taken with his unfortunate comrades to Libby Prison Richmond, but was left there sick when they went on to Andersonville Ga. Recovering, Mr. Bracewell was employed as a nurse in the prisoners' Hospital at Richmond, till in the autumn of 1864 he was parolled and exchanged, but did not return to his Reg. as his term of service had expired. The date of his discharge is Nov. 30. 1864. Mr. Bracewell returned to Athol in good health.

John S. Briggs, 27. Reg. (See page 126), went with his Reg. to Annapolis where he was sick with the Measles, but partially recovering went with his Reg. to North Carolina, was in the engagements at the capture of Roanoke Island and Newbern; was detailed to assist Surgeon Otis in the Hospital but upon his own request returned to the ranks; was again sick with the Asthma but recovering in part again assisted in the Hospital; but his health being permanently injured he was discharged July 29. 1862 and returned home. Mr. Briggs still suffers from the disease contracted in the service.

Francis B. Brock, 25. Reg. (See page 126), left Worcester with his Reg. Oct. 31. 1861 for Annapolis and went under Gen. Burnside to North Carolina; was in the battles at Roanoke Island, Newbern, Kinston, Whitehall and Goldsboro' N.

C. and in many other perilous expeditions in that State; went with the Reg. when it was ordered to Virginia and was with it in the engagements at Walthall Junction, Arrowfield Church and Drury's Bluff; went into the battle at Coal Harbor but was killed in it during the desperate but unavailing assault upon the enemy's works, June 3. 1864. His body lay upon the ground nearly or quite a week before it could be reached by our troops and buried. Mr. Brock's knapsack was left behind with others in Portsmouth and his Diary was recovered, the entries being brought down to within about a month of his death.

Henry D. Brock, 25. Reg. (See page 126), brother of the above, went with his Reg. to Annapolis Oct. 1861 and to N. Carolina under Gen. Burnside; was in the thickest of the fights at the capture of Roanoke Island and Newbern but soon after was taken sick and being declared unfit for duty was discharged, and returned home feeble, but gradually regained his health and strength.

John S. Brown, 57. Reg. (See page 134), first entered the service a member of Company 1. 25th Reg. from Orange and went with that Reg. to North Carolina; in the battle at the capture of Roanoke Island was very severely wounded in the head, a part of the scalp being raised from the bone which was replaced; but being unfit for duty he was discharged and returned home. Reentering the service in the 57. Reg. he went into camp with it at Worcester but his health not being good, he was discharged Oct. 15. 1864 before the Reg. left for the seat of war and returned home.

Walter R. Brown 34. Reg. (See page 130), went with his Reg. to Washington in Aug. 1862 and was with it in the numerous engagements in the Shenandoah valley, particularly at Charlestown Va. and in its vicinity in 1863 and in 1864 participated in the great battles at New Market, Piedmont, Lynchburg and Snicker's Gap. In the last mentioned engagement, Mr. Brown was taken prisoner and was confined at Danville Va. seven months, suffering greatly for want of food and from sickness. At length, he was parolled for exchange and reached Annapolis in Feb. 1865 very feeble, from which place he was sent to Worcester and was discharged from the Hospital there June 1. 1865, sixteen days before his term of service would have expired. Mr. Brown was residing in Spencer at the time of his enlistment and counted upon the quota for that Town, but belongs and now resides in Athol.

Daniel D. Bruce, 16. Reg. (See page 124), was among the number drafted from Athol July 1863 and was accepted and reported for service. Mr. Bruce joined his Reg. in Virginia and was in the service Twenty Two months. He was in the engagements at Mine Run, the Wilderness, Spottsylvania and Coal Harbor and also in the attack on the Weldon Rail Road. Late in the year 1864 Mr. Bruce was taken sick with Rheumatism and was in the City Point field Hospital, in one of the Hospitals at Annapolis and in the Chestnut Hill Hospital at Philadelphia till May 29. 1865 when he was discharged and returned home, feeble but gradually improving.

Thomas Burns, 53. Reg. (See page 131), went with his Reg. to Louisiana and participated in all its marches and engagements; was at the capture of Fort Bisland and in the assaults upon Port Hudson. Mr. Burns was one of the few of his company whose health remained good throughout the entire campaign of the 53. Reg. and he returned with it to Athol, Aug. 24. 1863.

George Carter, 21. Reg. (See page 125) went with his Reg. to Annapolis and early in 1862 to North Carolina under Gen. Burnside; was

in the battles which resulted in the capture of
Roanoke Island and of Newbern; was wounded in the leg in the last mentioned engagement;
came home on a furlough and partially recovering returned to his Regiment, but being as
it was supposed, permanently lame he was discharged Dec. 7. 1862. Mr. Carter has now
(Jan. 1866) in a great measure, recovered from
the effects of his wound.

Daniel Casavant, 53. Reg. (See page 132),
went with his Reg. to Louisiana, participated in
the capture of Fort Bisland and in the weary
marches to Opelousas and Alexandria and from
the latter place to Bayou Sara where he was
left sick; was removed to Baton Rouge where
he remained dangerously sick in the Hospital,
till the Reg. left for the North. His brother
Joseph Casavant of Athol went to Baton Rouge,
hoping to obtain his discharge and bring him
home, but was himself taken dangerously sick
at New Orleans and finally reached home a few
days before his brother returned with his Reg.
Daniel Casavant rejoined the Reg. Aug. 11.
1863 and returned home with it, very sick, suffering greatly throughout the long journey; but
after a few weeks began to recover and at
length was restored to perfect health.

John M. Casavant, 32. Reg. (See page 130), joined this Reg. when it was the First Battalion at Fort Warren and remained with it till the spring of 1862, when receiving a furlough to come home, he disappeared, and never returned to his Regiment.

Adin W. Caswell, 27. Reg. (See page 126), was commissioned Captain of Comp. B which he had recruited in Athol and vicinity in the autumn of 1861 and was at the head of it during the three years of his service. He went with his Reg. to North Carolina and remained with it without any furlough till the time of his discharge, leading his company in nearly every engagement, and never asking a man to go where he was not ready to lead. He was sick at the capture of Roanoke Island, but was at the head of his company at Newbern, Kinston, Whitehall, Goldsboro' and in the famous defence of Washington N. C. At Gum Swamp he commanded three Companies that were sent to prevent an attack in the rear, and succeeded in capturing the baggage train of the enemy and some prisoners. He was at the head of his Company during the campaign in Virginia but was sick (having been poisoned) at the time of the disastrous conflict at Drury's Bluff. He was engaged at Coal Harbor where he was struck by a piece of a shell between his shoulders and prostrated but not dangerously wounded. After the death of Major Walker at Coal Harbor, who commanded the Reg. after the capture of his superior officers, Capt. Caswell was in command of the Reg. for about ten weeks, and for a shorter time at a later period. He came out of the fight at Coal Harbor with his overcoat pierced by bullets in many places but not severely wounded. He had previously received a slight wound at Port Walthall. At the close of his term of service Capt. Caswell returned home in health.

Lyman A. Chamberlain, 27. Reg. (See page 126), went with the Reg. to Annapolis and was sick there with the Measles but recovered sufficiently to go to North Carolina and to participate in the capture of Roanoke Island. This was the only engagement in which Mr. Chamberlain took part as he was sick at the capture of Newbern and not long after went into the Hospital at Beaufort N. Carolina. Recovering he remained in the Hospital as nurse and at a later period was Ward Master in the same, till the term of his enlistment having expired he was discharged and came home in good health.

Warren E. Chamberlain, 36. Reg. (See page

14

131), went with the Reg, in Sept. 1862 to Washington and from that city into service in Maryland and Virginia; was with his Reg. which was held in reserve at the battle of Fredericksburg and went with it to Cincinnati and Lexington Kentucky; afterwards went to Mississippi and was with the Reg. at Jackson and in the rear of Vicksburg at the time of its capture; returned to Kentucky and had a furlough Sept. 24. 1863 and not returning, was reported by the authorities of the Commonwealth to the Selectmen of Athol as a deserter.

Ephraim F. Chase, 53. Reg. (See page 132), went with his Reg. to Louisiana in Jan. 1863 and after participating in the capture of Fort Bisland and in the marches to Opelousas and Alexandria was sent back sick from the last mentioned place to Brashear City where he was taken prisoner by the enemy June 23. 1863; was carried to Ship Island for exchange July 9. rejoined his Company Aug. 11. and returned with it to Athol Aug. 24. 1863.

Frederic A. Chubb, 32. Reg. (See page 130), joined this Reg. when it was the First Battalion in Fort Warren and went with it to Washington and Harrison's Landing Va.; was taken sick and sent to the Hospital; came home on a fur-

lough and partially recovering went to a Hospital in New York, but not being deemed able
to return to his Reg. was discharged Feb. 10.
1863 and came home.

John S. Clark, of the Navy. (See page 135).
Mr. Clark was formerly a Captain in the Mer-
chant Service but when the Rebellion broke
out was a farmer in Athol. Sept. 20. 1862 he
was examined and approved as Acting Ensign
in the Navy, and sent on board the Macedonia
for instruction. In Nov. of the same year he
was detached from this ship and sent to the
West Gulf Squadron commanded by Admiral
Farragut, and Jan. 1. 1863 he was on duty on
board the Sloop of War Preble at Pensacola.
April 27. this ship took fire and blew up and
Mr. Clark lost all his outfit and valuable nautical
instruments. He was then assigned to the Fri-
gate Potomac at Pensacola, and at a later period
to the U. S. Steamer Calhoun, and was in the
naval assault upon Fort Powell, Mobile, in Feb.
1864, when the Sawyers' Shells were used most
effectively. Mr. Clark was at that time executive officer of the Calhoun which was the Flag
Ship, having been promoted for good conduct,
and he was soon sent in command of the Calhoun to New Orleans, for repairs. But this ship
having been sold, he was given command of the

U. S. Steamer Pampero, Guard Ship at the South West Pass, and was in this service two months, when he went on board the Sloop of War Portsmouth, Guard Ship of New Orleans. Desiring more active service Mr. Clark was next placed in command of the Yacht Schooner Corypheus to cruise in Lake Pontchartrain when the Yellow Fever broke out among the crew and most of them were sent to the Hospital. Mr. Clark was next engaged in a successful effort to raise the sunken Steamer Narcissus in Mobile Harbor and picking up torpedoes under the guns of the enemy. In this last mentioned employment he was engaged for nine days. Soon after the surrender of Mobile Mr. Clark had a furlough to come home, and received an honorable discharge from the service in Nov. 1865. He had been more than three years in constant and hard service and had been on board ten vessels of the Navy four of which he had had the honor to command. Ten days he was engaged in the bombardment of Fort Powell and in many other perilous enterprises, and it is not surprising that he came out of the service feeble. At this time (Jan. 1866) he is especially suffering from impaired eyesight.

John Clark, 27. Reg. (See page 126), went with his Reg. to North Carolina and was in the engagements at Roanoke Island, Newbern, Kinston, Whitehall and Goldsboro'; was in service at the siege of Washington N. C. and after participating in the engagement at Gum Swamp went with his Regiment to Va. and was detailed to guard prisoners at Norfolk Va. during the engagements at Drury's Bluff and Coal Harbor. During the first years of the war, Mr. Clark counted upon the quota of Phillipston but re-enlisted Jan. 1864 from Athol, and in the desperate fight in which the 27th Reg. was engaged March 18. 1865 near Kinston N. Carolina he was severely wounded in the right cheek, left arm and side and taken prisoner with nearly all his comrades; was carried to Richmond, paroled for exchange and reached Annapolis March 27. As soon as he was able he came home and has been for nine months gradually recovering. Mr. Clark was discharged June 20. 1865, having served in our army nearly four years, and in the army of Great Britain five years before coming to the United States.

George H. Clark, 32. Reg. (See page 130) joined the 1st Battalion at Fort Warren early in the year 1862 and went with it as the 32d Reg. to Harrison's Landing Va. was in the campaign in Maryland, in the battle at Antietam and afterwards in the severe conflicts at Fredericksburg,

14*

and Chancellorsville; came to Pennsylvania
when that State was invaded by Lee's army in
1863 and was in the thickest of the fight at
Gettysburg, returned with his Reg. to Virginia
and was in the battles in the Wilderness, at Laurel Hill, at Tolopotamy Creek and in front of
Petersburg till late in the year 1864 when he
was taken sick of Chronic Diarrhœa; and having been removed to the U. S. General Hospital
Amory Square, Washington, he died there Dec.
15. 1864. Mr. Clark was buried in Washington.
The 32. Reg. was in twenty one battles during
the year before he was taken sick and he is supposed to have been in all of them.

William L. Clutterbuck, 2. Reg. (See page 122),
was among the first that volunteered and went
into the service from Athol; went with his Reg.
in July 1861 from Camp Andrew West Roxbury
to Maryland and from thence to Virginia, but
while at Martinsburg, losing one of his thumbs
by an accidental discharge of his musket as he
declared, he was discharged Sept. 1861 from the
service and returned home.

Edward P. Clapp, 53. Reg. (See page 132),
went with his Reg. to Louisiana, and was detailed
Fifer for Company E; was with the Reg. at the
capture of Fort Bisland and during the marches

to Opelousas and Alexandria and in all the attacks that resulted in the capture of Port Hudson. Mr. Clapp enjoyed good health during the whole campaign and returned with his Company to Athol Aug. 24. 1863.

Welcome J. Cleaveland, 53. Reg. (See page 132), went with his Reg. to Louisiana but before Gen· Banks moved his forces against the enemy was taken sick with the measles ; was three months in the Hospital, but deemed himself able to go with his Reg. and to engage in the first day's fight near Brashear City ; but the effort proved too much for him as he was immediately taken worse and died at Brashear City April 24. 1863. Mr. Cleaveland's remains were removed to New Orleans for burial, and funeral services were attended in Athol May 17. in the church of the Evangelical Society.

Cyrus W. Conant, 53. Reg. (See page 132), went with his Reg. in Jan. 1863 to Louisiana and when the forces moved against the enemy he accompanied them in the first engagements, but being taken sick at Vermillionville La. he was sent to Brashear City April 19, and at a later period was carried to the United States Barracks Hospital New Orleans where he died July 10. 1863. His disease was Chronic Diarrhœa. It

was impracticable to bring the remains of Mr.
Conant home for burial, but friendship has in-
scribed his name upon a beautiful Granite Shaft
in the Cemetery at Athol.

Artemas W. Conant, 53. Reg. (See page 132),
brother of the above, went with his Reg. in the
Banks Expedition to Louisiana and was with his
Company in the engagements near Brashear
City and in the long marches to Opelousas and
Alexandria and back to the Mississippi River,
also in the assaults upon Port Hudson. The
health of Mr. Conant was good during the whole
Campaign so that he was constantly in service,
and returned with his Company to Athol Aug.
24. 1863.

James Connell, 32. Reg. (See page 130), joined
the Reg. when it was the First Battalion at Fort
Warren, and went with it to Washington and to
Harrison's Landing Va.; was taken sick at the
latter place and removed with the sick to Philadelphia; was in a Hospital there some months
but partially recovering was sent to Alexandria
Va. where as soon as he was able to labor he was
employed in building barracks. After he had
wholly recovered he rejoined his Reg. and was
with it in service during the latter part of the
year 1863. In Jan. 1864 he reenlisted and

came home on a furlough of thirty days. Returning to his Reg. with the reenlisted men in Feb. he remained with his Company at Liberty Va. till the last of April 1864, when the grand movement under Gen. Grant commenced. Mr. Connell was in the great battle of the Wilderness May 5. and in the battle of Laurel Hill May 12. and was instantly killed not far from Spottsylvania Court House. Mr. Connell was shot in the morning and his remains lay upon the breast works till evening when they were recovered and buried by his comrade Ebenezer Kneeland and others.

Joseph H. Collins, 21. Reg. (See page 125), went with the Reg. to Annapolis and to North Carolina, was in the engagements at Roanoke Island, Newbern, Camden and in the forced march to Pollocksville to rescue the 2d Maryland Reg.; went with his Reg. to Virginia in July 1862, was in the Bull Run battle No. 2. when Gen. Pope's campaign in Virginia ended; was in the battles at Chantilly and Antietam and finally in the great contest at Fredericksburg Dec. 12. 1862. Mr. Collins had been Color-Corporal but was, in the last mentioned engagement, Color Sergeant, and when about sixty rods from the City Fredericksburg, he was severely wounded in the leg below the knee and fell. It was then that Ser-

geant Plunkett of Company E seized the colors
and was bearing them forward when a shell from
the rebel earth works carried away both of his
arms.   Mr. Collins was removed among the
wounded to one of the Hospitals at Washington
where he died of his wound Jan. 3. 1863.   His
remains were brought North by his Widow and
buried at Southboro' Mass. Jan. 12. 1863.

Marshall Collins, 53. Reg. (See page 132), went
with the Company under Capt. Fay to Louisiana
in Jan. 1863 and was with his Reg. in the capture of Fort Bisland and in the long marches to
Opelousas and Alexandria and back to the Mississippi River: was sent sick with Chronic Diarrhœa from before Port Hudson, June 6. 1863 to
Baton Rouge where he died in a little more than
a month, viz. July 14. 1863.   Mr. Collins was
buried at Baton Rouge, and left in Athol a wife
and two children.

Vernon S. Cook, 11. Reg. (See page 123), entered the service June 13. 1861 and was in the
battles at Yorktown, Williamsburg, Fair Oaks,
Savage's Station, Glendale, Malvern Hill and
others when Gen. McClellan moved upon Richmond.   Afterwards he participated in the engagements at Bull Run No. 2. Chantilly, Fredericksburg, Chancellorsville, Gettysburg, Manassas,

Rappahannock, Locust Grove and Mine Run. Having reenlisted he was, in 1864, in the engagements before Petersburg, on the South Side Rail Road and at the time of the Weldon Rail Road Raid as well as at Hatcher's Run. Soon after the last mentioned engagement Mr. Cook was taken sick and sent to a Hospital at Washington, when being deemed unfit for longer service he was discharged June 9. 1865. He returned home and regained his health.

Linus Crawford, 27. Reg. (See page 126), went with his Reg. to Annapolis and North Carolina ; was in the battles at Roanoke Island, Newbern, Kinston, Whitehall and Goldsboro', but in Nov. 1862 his health failed, and not regaining it he was discharged, because of disability, June 22. 1863 and returned to Athol. Mr. Crawford was Cook for his Company a part of the time of his service.

Joel B. Cummings, 21. Reg. (see page 125), went with his Reg. to Annapolis and in the Burnside Expedition to North Carolina ; was in the battles at Roanoke Island and at Newbern, in the latter of which he was severely wounded in the shoulder, the ball penetrating so deep that it was impossible to extract it. Being, of course, unfit for service, Mr. Cummings returned to

Athol with Laban Morse Esqr. in April 1862. During the summer following, his health improved, but it was not deemed best that he should return to his Reg. and he was discharged Nov. 10. 1862. Since his discharge Mr. Cummings has nearly regained his health, though the ball which is still in the vicinity of his lungs is, at times, quite troublesome.

Frederic Cummings, 2. Reg. (See page 122), was among the first who went into the service from Athol joining his Regiment at West Roxbury in May 1861. Went with his Reg. to Maryland and into the bloody engagements in the Shenandoah Valley, but after a service of about sixteen months he was taken sick and was discharged at Sharpsburg Maryland. This was soon after the battle at Antietam. Mr. Cummings recovered after his return.

Henry N. Darling, 27. Reg. (See page 127), was among the recruits that joined this Reg. in North Carolina in the autumn of 1862 and was with it in the engagements at Kinston, Whitehall and Goldsboro' as also in the famous defeat of the enemy in the siege of Washington N. C. and May 1863 was detailed to serve in the Engineer Corps in which he remained till his term of service expired, first in North Carolina and at

a later period in Virginia. Mr. Darling is at
this time, Jan. 1866, in Texas with the army,
but not in a military capacity.

Azor S. Davis, 25. Reg. (See page 126), enlisted
as a Musician Aug. 1862 and was assigned to the
25. Reg. but was detailed to perform duty at
Camp Day Cambridge till Jan. 24. 1863 when he
went to Fort Independence Boston Harbor for a
short time. Being then sent to Newbern N. C.
he joined his Reg. in Feb. 1863 and remained at
Newbern till Oct. of the same year when he went
to Newport News Va. meanwhile going on various expeditions in North Carolina and Virginia.
In the Spring of 1864 Mr. Davis with his Reg.
joined the Army of the James, went to Bermuda
Hundred and afterwards moved towards Petersburg, was in the engagements at Walthall Junction, Drury's Bluff and Coal Harbor and finally
in the siege of Petersburg. In Sept. 1864 he
went back to Newbern, came home to be discharged and was mustered out of the service at
the expiration of his term of enlistment Oct. 20.
1864. Mr. Davis was sick but little while in the
army and returned home in good health.

Otis E. Davis, 34. Reg. (See page 136), joined
the Reg. when it was organized and went with it
to Maryland and Virginia and was with it in va-

rious services before it was in any decisive engagement with the enemy; was in the battle of Berryville Oct. 1863 under Gen. Sigel; of Piedmont June 1864 under Gen. Hunter; near Lynchburg in the same month, at Snicker's Gap, July 1864; at Winchester Sept. 1864 under Gen. Sheridan and under the same at Fisher's Hill two days later; was wounded by a shell near Cedar Creek Va. and taken prisoner Oct. 13. 1864; reached Libby Prison Richmond Oct. 27.; was taken sick with the Typhoid Fever and removed to the Prison Hospital Nov. 9.; was very sick, but after six weeks began to gain, till finally his health was in a good degree restored. But though nearly well he was permitted to remain in the Hospital till he was paroled for exchange, Feb. 5. 1865. Mr. Davis reached Annapolis Feb. 7. and came home on a furlough Feb. 20., having been treated on the whole more kindly than most of the prisoners. He returned to Annapolis but was in no other engagements, and was discharged with his Reg. June 16, 1865.

Patrick Dempsey, 9. Reg. (See page 123), was the only man from Athol that served three full years with this renowned Reg.; went with it to the seat of war and was with it in the following engagements as appears from the indorsement upon his discharge papers, Yorktown, Siege of Yorktown, Hanover Court House, Mechanicsville, Gains' Mill, Malvern, Chickahominy, Hanover Landing, Bull Run No. 2, Botelers' Mills, Antietam, Shepardstown, Fredericksburg, Chancellorsville, Brandy Station, Gettysburg, Wapping Heights, Rappahannock Station, Bristol Station, Mine Run, the Wilderness, Spottsylvania, North Anna, Cedar Grove and Shady Oak Grove; twenty five battles in all, to say nothing of many other engagements less decisive.   Mr. Dempsey was discharged June 21st 1864 by reason of the expiration of his term of service, and returned home in health, and as it appears, with an honorable record.

Anthony V. Dimock, 53. Reg. (See page 132), went with his Company under Capt. Fay to Louisiana; was sick with a Fever at Algiers La. and left sick there when Gen. Banks moved his forces against the enemy; was a part of the time in a Hospital at New Orleans, but was not able to be in any of the engagements of his Reg.; rejoined it Aug. 11. 1863 and returned with it Aug. 24. with his health improved.

George S. Dresser, 27. Reg. (See page 127), joined the Reg. with the second Company of recruits from Athol in the autumn of 1863; took

part in the expedition to Suffolk Va. in April
1864, and was doubtless in the engagements at
Port Walthall and Arrowfield Church. Mr. Dresser
was taken prisoner with most of his comrades in
the disastrous conflict at Drury's Bluff May 16.
1864, was removed to Libby Prison Richmond
and thence to Danville where he was taken sick
of Lung Fever. He was afterwards carried to
Andersonville Ga. where he was left very sick
when his comrades were removed to other
prisons, and doubtless died there in the summer
or autumn of 1864, a victim of rebel cruelty.

George W. Drury Jr., 53. Reg. (See page 132),
went with his Reg. to Louisiana; was taken sick
while the Reg. was at Camp Kearney Carrolton
and was left there when it moved; was not
present in the first engagements with the enemy,
but was able to rejoin his Company at Alexandria
to march with it upon Port Hudson, and to take
part in the reduction of that place. Mr. Drury
returned in comfortable health with his Reg.
Aug. 24. 1863.

Simeon S. Drury, 53. Reg. (See page 132),
brother of the above; went with his Reg. to
Louisiana and participated in all its engagements
and marches from the beginning to the end of
the Campaign, and returned with his Reg. in

good health, Aug. 24. 1863. At a later period, viz. in the Spring of 1865, Mr. Drury returned to the United States Service under a Contract for six months which he spent in the vicinity of Chattanooga Tennessee, serving as Master's Mate on board a number of United States Boats in the Tennessee River, and came home in health at the expiration of his engagement.

John Doyle, 36. Reg. (See page 131), went with his Reg. to Virginia and was with it when it was sent to Kentucky and at a later period to Mississippi; was in the engagements at Jackson Miss. and in all the work and suffering in the rear of Vicksburg during the siege and capture of that place; returned with his Reg. to Kentucky and was in the engagements that saved Knoxville Tenn. from the Rebels; was with the Reg. when it returned to Virginia and became a part of the army of Gen. Grant when he moved towards Richmond; was in the battles of the Wilderness and at Spottsylvania and before Petersburg where he was taken prisoner Sept. 30. 1864 having been severely wounded in the hand by a ball passing through it. Mr. Doyle was carried first to Richmond where he was robbed of two months pay, clothing &c. and thence was sent to the Prison at Salisbury N. Carolina, where he suffered greatly through lack

15*

of food and clothing.   After five months and ten days he was paroled for exchange and sent to Annapolis, very feeble.   From Annapolis he came home on a furlough, but being crippled by his wound which has caused him to lose the use of one finger, and worn out by the rigors of his imprisonment he was not sent back to his Reg., but was discharged June 22. 1865.

Theodore Jones Dyer, 25. Reg. (See page 126), went with his Reg. to North Carolina and assisted in the captures of Roanoke Island and Newbern, was. in the engagements at Kinston, Whitehall and Goldsboro' and in all the expeditions of his Regiment in North Carolina, went with his Reg. to Virginia and was doubtless in the engagements at Arrowfield Church, Drury's Bluff and Coal Harbor, but during the protracted siege of Petersburg he was taken sick and died near that city Sept. 19. 1864.   We have but few of the particulars respecting Mr. Dyer's last year of service or of his death.

John D. Emerson, 2. Reg. (See page 122), was in the Company of the young men that went into the service of the Government under the first call for troops; was sick during a part of the early campaign of his Reg. in Maryland and Virginia, but recovering, was detached from his

Reg. and ordered to Darnstown Md. to await orders from the chief of the Signal Corps; after five weeks was sent to Georgetown D. C. and entered the School for Signal Instruction in that City; went South with the Expedition of Gen. W. T. Sherman when the Forts of Port Royal S. C. were captured, was on board the Steamer Oriental with Gen. Viale and Staff during the assault; landed at Port Royal and did Signal duty there and in that vicinity a few weeks and was then located at Beaufort S. C.; in 1863 was under Gen. Gillmore on Morris Island and a part of the time had charge of a Telegraph leading from a bomb proof within three hundred yards of Fort Wagner; was on duty in the bomb-proof when a shell from the Fort penetrated it and exploded; was almost buried in the sand and was taken out, senseless and as it was thought mortally wounded, was carried to Beaufort and was restored to reason and speech in eight days and to a good measure of health in a few weeks; returned to duty on Morris Island and was on board the Ironsides when the fleet attacked Fort Sumter; went in 1864 under Gen. Seymour to Florida and remained there till Gen. Gillmore was ordered to reinforce Gen. Butler in Virginia when he joined the Army of the James and was with it doing Signal duty in some of its severest conflicts, till the time for which he had enlisted,

expired when he was discharged and came home.
After a few months, Mr. Emerson reentered the
service in the 2d New York Heavy Artillery in
which he remained till the end of the war or 8½
months.   His Reg. belonged to the Army of the
Potomac and was in the terrible fighting which
resulted in the fall of Richmond and the surrender of Gen. Lee's army.   Soon after joining
this Reg. Mr. Emerson was detailed as Chief
Clerk in the Adjutant's office and served in this
capacity, having received a 2d Lieutenant's Commission from the Governor of New York and
when his Reg. was mustered out of service he
returned home in health.

Farwell F. Fay, 53. Reg. (See page 131),
recruited in Aug. 1862 Company E of the 53.
Reg. in Athol and vicinity; was chosen Captain
of said Company Sept. 13. 1862 and Commissioned by the Governor of the Commonwealth
five days later; went into Camp with his Company at Groton Junction Oct. 1. and to New
York Nov. 30.; sailed for Louisiana Jan. 1863
and went into Camp at Carrollton; was at the
head of his Company at the capture of Fort
Bisland and during all the marches to Opelousas
and Alexandria and to the rear of Port Hudson;
led his Company in the assault upon Port Hudson of June 14. which failed through no fault of

the 53d Regiment or of any of its Officers; two days later, viz. June 16. was appointed Acting Major of the Reg. and two days later still was placed in Command of the same, in which capacity he acted till after the surrender of Port Hudson, viz. till July 12. at which time he was taken sick and removed to the Officers Hospital at Baton Rouge. He was sick at Baton Rouge fifteen days when he entered St. Louis Hospital New Orleans where he remained till orders came to collect the sick and prepare to leave for the North. Capt. Fay rejoined the Reg. Aug. 10. 1863 and returned to Massachusetts at the head of his Company Aug. 24. of the same year, with health somewhat impaired but gradually improving.

In July 1864, Capt. Fay was commissioned as Assistant Adjutant General of Massachusetts, to recruit for the Commonwealth in the Department of Mississippi and by Special Orders No. 12. bearing date July 23. 1864 was assigned to the Staff of Lieut. Col. Eli C. Kinsley and directed to proceed with him to Vicksburg Miss. Capt. Fay entered upon this difficult service and was eminently successful; but in Nov. 1864 he tendered his resignation on account of sickness in his family; and this being accepted he was honorably discharged Dec. 8. 1864.

William G. Fay, 53. Reg. (See page 132),
went with his Reg. to New York was detailed
for duty on board the Ship "Belle Wood" Jan.
8. 1863, joined his Reg. again in Feb. and was
with it in all its engagements and marches till
after the surrender of Port Hudson when he was
left sick at the Convalescent Camp at Baton
Rouge.   Mr. Fay left for home on board the St.
Mary's Aug. 7. reached New York Aug. 14. and
Athol Aug. 19. 1863, feeble but gradually improving.

Freeborn R. Fay, 53. Reg. (See page 132),
brother of the above, was advised by the Surgeon
of the Reg. at Camp Stevens to ask for a discharge because of an organic affection of the
heart, but was so anxious to go into the service
that he could not follow this advice; was detailed
at New York for service on board the Ship
"Belle Wood" and after arriving in Louisiana
was made the Surgeon's Orderly, went with the
Reg. in its various engagements and marches,
was injured by being thrown from a wagon near
Port Hudson and went into the Hospital at Baton Rouge; left for Massachusetts with a part of
the sick men on board the St. Mary's Aug. 7. arrived at New York Aug. 14. and reached home,
in feeble health, but recovering, Aug. 20. 1863.
Mr. Fay died suddenly of organic disease of the
heart, at Athol May 4. 1865.

Levi B. Fay, 53. Reg. (See page 132), went with his Company into Camp at Groton Junction and was made Corporal Oct. 17. 1862; was with the Reg. in good health in the engagements near Brashear City, in all 'its marches and fighting before Port Hudson, and indeed in every kind of service required of it during its entire campaign in Louisiana and Mississippi, and returned with it to Massachusetts Aug. 24. 1863.

Joseph F. Fay, 27. Reg. (See page 128), belonged to the Regimental Band and accompanied his Reg. to North Carolina and was with it in the battles at Roanoke Island and Newbern, but after serving about one year in this capacity was discharged by reason of the Government Order discontinuing Regimental Bands and returned to Athol.

Charles D. Fisher, 36. Reg. (See page 131), went with his regiment to Washington and into service in various movements in Maryland and Virginia; passed over to Parkersburg in West Virginia and down the Ohio to Lexington Ky. went with his Reg. to guard the Polls at Cincinnati and thence to participate in the capture of Vicksburg under Gen. Grant; was in the engagement at Jackson Miss. and after the fall of Vicksburg returned to Kentucky detailed as

nurse for the sick soldiers but was himself soon
sick through incessant labor and ulcerations in
his limbs; was sent to the Hospital at Camp
Dennison Ohio where he remained nearly two
months when he had a furlough and came home.
Thorough examinations at a later date at Boston
proved Mr. Fisher unfit for service in the field
and he was discharged Nov. 19. 1863. His disease continued for many months, but he gradually improved in health, and has nearly recovered.

Leyton W. Follett, 53. Reg. (See page 132),
went with his Reg. to Louisiana, was always fit
for duty and always present in its marches and
engagements, participated in the captures of
Fort Bisland and Port Hudson, and returned to
Athol in health Aug. 24. 1863.

Azro B. Folsom, 53. Reg. (See page 132),
went with his Reg. to Louisiana and was with it
when Gen. Banks moved against the forces of
the enemy in April 1863, was detailed for special
duty in the Quartermaster's Department April
27. 1863; rejoined the Company Aug. 9. and
returned with it, feeble but convalescent, Aug.
24. 1863.

Daniel W. Foster, 36. Reg. (See page 131),

went with his Reg. to Washington and was with
with it in various services in Maryland and Virginia; was taken severely sick with an intermit-
tent fever on board the Transport South Amer-
ica in Chesapeake Bay; was landed at Newport
News and died in the Hospital there Feb. 14.
1863; was buried there but his remains were disinterred by his Brother W. H. Foster and brought
to Athol. Funeral Services were held in the
church of the 1st Cong. Society, Athol, Feb. 26.
1863.

Elmer G. Foster, 1st Battalion (See page 130),
joined this Battalion before it became the 32.
Reg. at Fort Warren in Feb. 1862 but in a few
days was taken sick and discharged as unfit for
service Feb. 20. 1862. Mr. Foster returned to
Athol feeble and continued feeble till Feb. 28.
1864 when he died; never having recovered
from the sickness that came upon him during
the few days he was in service at Fort Warren.

Columbus Fox, 2d Reg. (See page 122), was
among the first men who went into the Army
from Athol, was with his Reg. in various engagements and services in Maryland and Virginia, particularly in the advance and retreat of
Gen. Banks in the Shenandoah Valley; was in
the battle at Gettysburg Pa.; went with his Reg.

16

to Kentucky and Tennessee and was in various
engagements in those States, remaining with his
Reg. four months or more after the period of his
enlistment had expired, because the Reg. was
almost constantly in battle, in the vicinity of
Atlanta Ga. After his discharge and return
home in health Mr. Fox reentered the service in
the New York 3d Cavalry for one year, but after
serving nine months, the war closed and he was
discharged.

Patrick W. Fox, 21. and 57. Reg. (See page
125), went with the 21. Reg. in the Burnside Expedition to North Carolina and was in the battles at Roanoke Island, Newbern and Camden
in the last mentioned of which he was wounded
in the arm. He was also wounded in the hand
and partially disabled by accident. In the battle of Chantilly he was wounded in the foot but
escaped wounds in the 2d Bull Run fight. Being unfit to continue in the service because of
his wounds, he was honorably discharged Feb.
14. 1863. Mr. Fox was made Corporal March
16. 1862. His wounds having healed Mr Fox
reentered the service in the 57. Reg. having
been Sergeant of Guard at the office of Pro.
Marshal at Greenfield.

In the battle of the Wilderness he was
wounded in the head, but was in the engage-

ment at Spottsylvania before going into the Hospital at Washington. Rejoining his Reg. he was detailed as one of the Independent Mounted Scouts, having been promoted Sergeant in the battle of the Wilderness. As a Scout he had charge of thirteen men and was engaged every night in this service. On one occasion when attacked by Mosby, he lost four of his men. But the service proving too hard for him, he was taken sick and was two months again in the Hospital. Partially recovering, he was transferred April 5. 1865 to the Veteran Reserve Corps and was honorably discharged Aug. 24. 1865. Mr. Fox received four wounds in all, one of which made him lame in the ankle joint and another entirely disabled two of his fingers, and when he at length returned home, he brought the most honorable testimonials to his fidelity and courage.

Byron A. French, 2. and 53. Reg. (See page 122), was among the first men who enlisted from Athol joining the 2. Reg. Col. Gordon at West Roxbury ; went with his Reg. to the Upper Potomac and while in service there received a wound in the hand at Darnstown Maryland which disabled him for the time and he was discharged Dec. 1. 1861. Recovering the use of his hand, he entered the 53. Reg., was made Or derly Sergeant of Comp. E Oct. 17. 1862; went with the Regiment to Louisiana; was in the fight at Fort Bisland; was left sick at Vermillionville La. April 19. 1863: rejoined his Company at Alexandria, was in all the engagements at the capture of Port Hudson and returned to Athol Aug. 24. 1863. Mr. French entered the service for the third time and was sent to the school for Signal instruction at Georgetown D. C. where he remained a number of months, and was with the Signal Corps at Fort Stevens near Washington during the summer of 1865 when he was mustered out of the service.

Van Buren French, 27. Reg. (See page 127), went with his Reg. into service in North Carolina and was in the engagements at Roanoke Island and Newbern; was wounded in the latter by a spent ball that struck his arm; returned to Athol with Laban Morse Esq. in April 1862 on a furlough; but being deemed unfit for service he was discharged Sept. 24. 1862. Mr. French was made Corporal, Oct. 1861. At a later period he reentered the service in the 2d Heavy Artillery, Comp. B; went to North Carolina, was sick in the Hospital at Newbern three months and finally discharged for disability.

William A. Fry, 32. Reg. (See page 130), was

at Fort Warren and went with the Reg. to
Washington and to Harrison's Landing; was
with the Reg. in service in Maryland and returned with it to Virginia; was taken sick near
Centreville Va. and was sent into one of the
Hospitals at Washington where he remained
nearly nine months; was also in a Hospital
for a short time in New York; recovering, returned to his Reg. in Virginia in season to participate in the advance under Gen. Grant in May
1864; passed safely through the battles of the
Wilderness, Spottsylvania, Tolopotomy Swamp.
Bethesda Church, in front of Petersburg June
18., on the Weldon Rail Road and at Preble's
Farm, when having served three years he was
discharged Nov. 25. 1864 and returned to Athol
in health.

Sumner S. Giles, 30. Reg. (See page 129), went
South with his Reg. under Gen. Butler and took
an active part in the various battles in the vicinity of New Orleans and before Port Hudson;
was wounded in the right hand in the fight at
Donaldsonville La. and being disabled by his
wound for four months was discharged Oct. 24.
1863 and returned to Athol. Towards the close
of the war Mr. Giles reentered the service in
the 13th Reg. Vet. Reserve Corps, but was not
sent out of New England and was finally di-

charged Oct. 24. 1865, having served fourteen months.

Alfred Goddard, 53. Reg. (See page 132), went with his Reg. into service in Louisiana and was with it in the capture of Fort Bisland and upon all the marches till the forces of Gen. Banks reached Opelousas where he was taken sick and sent back to Brashear City May 5. 1863. At Brashear City Mr. Goddard was taken prisoner June 23.; sixteen days later was sent to Ship Island for exchange; returned to New Orleans Aug. 5.: rejoined his Company Aug. 11. and returned home with it in comfortable health Aug. 24. 1863.

Charles Virgil Goddard, 53. Reg. (See page 132), went with his Reg. to Louisiana and was wounded in the thigh during the first engagement, viz. at the capture of Fort Bisland; reluctantly went to the rear and was sent into the Hospital where he remained till July, 4. 1863 when he rejoined his Company and returned with it to Massachusetts, among the sick, but gradually gained till his health was perfectly restored.

Jacob Orlando Gould, 53. Reg. (See page 132), went into service in Louisiana and was with his

Reg. in the fight at Fort Bisland and in the long and tedious marches to Opelousas and Alexandria, was left sick at Bayou Sara May 23. 1873; was removed to the United States General Hospital at Baton Rouge, where he died July 27. 1863 of Chronic Diarrhea. Mr. Gould had been made Corporal May 1. 1863 in the place of Corporal George W. Knights deceased.

Charles S. Green, 2. Reg. (See page 122), was in the company of young men who first enlisted from Athol in the spring of 1861; went into camp at West Roxbury and with his Reg. into service on the Upper Potomac; was wagoner and in the engagements in Gen. Bank's advance and retreat in the Shenandoah Valley; in Dec. 1862 was taken dangerously sick of brain Fever and died at Frederick City Maryland Dec. 20. 1862. His remains were sent to his friends by his comrades, one of whom Leander W. Phelps of Athol had been detailed to take care of him in the Hospital.

Charles Gray, 27. Reg. (See page 127), went with the Reg. into service in North Carolina having been made Sergeant Oct. 1. 1861; was engaged at the capture of Roanoke Island and in the battles of Kinston, Whitehall and Goldsboro'; served in the defence of Washington N. C. and

in the engagement at Gum Swamp; went with
his Regiment to Virginia and was in the fights
at Port Walthall, Arrowfield Church and Drury's Bluff; was taken prisoner in the last mentioned engagement with a large part of his
Regiment; was in Libby Prison, Richmond, one
week; was taken thence to Andersonville Ga.;
from Andersonville to Savannah, from Savannah
to Millen and from Millen back to Savannah,
being in prison in these places nearly six
months; was generally well, though he suffered
like his unfortunate comrades for food and
water; was finally paroled for exchange Nov.
25. 1864 and next day went on board a transport for Annapolis; had a furlough for 30 days
and reached Athol Dec. 17. 1864; returned to
Annapolis Jan. 14. 1865 and served in the Engineer Corps there from Feb. 13. till May 3.; went
back to Newbern and rejoined his Reg. June 5.;
was mustered out of the service with his Reg.
June 26. 1865. and returned in health to Athol.
Mr. Gray reenlisted Jan. 1. 1864.

Charles E. Hager, 21. Reg. (See page 125),
went with his Reg. into service in North Carolina and was in the engagements at Roanoke Island, Newbern, Camden and other places in that
State, but at a later period (supposed to be
while the 21. Reg. was in service in Virginia,) he

was thrown from a horse in Alexandria Va. and killed. The particular circumstances and precise date of his death, the Committee in charge of this Record have not been able to learn.

Seth F. Hale, 21. Reg. (See page 125), went with his Reg. into service in North Carolina and was in the engagements at Roanoke Island, Newbern and Camden in that State; also at Chantilly Va. and at South Mountain and Antietam Md.; in the last mentioned battle was severely wounded in the right foot and was in various Hospitals in Maryland under treatment till June 17. 1863 when he was transferred to the Veteran Reserve Corps and put on duty as Orderly at the Provost Marshal's Office in Baltimore and afterwards served in the same capacity in Washington at Head Quarters; in April 1864 made application to rejoin his Reg. which then belonged to the Army of the Potomac, and was in season to participate in the Battles of the Wilderness and Spottsylvania; May 12 was again severely wounded in the left hip, was removed to the Harewood Hospital at Washington and from thence to Worcester where he was mustered out of service Aug. 30. 1864, the term of his enlistment having expired. Mr. Hale has recovered from the effects of the wounds he received. In May 1865 he received a Commission as 2d Lieutenant in the Militia of the Commonwealth.

James A. Hand, 31. Reg. (See page 129), went with the Reg. as a part of Maj. Gen. Butler's Expedition to Ship Island and afterwards participated in the capture of New Orleans and in the engagements under Gen. Banks in Louisiana and also in the capture of Port Hudson. In 1863 Mr. Hand's health failed, and after remaining in the Hospital a number of months, he was discharged Nov. 5. of that year and came home. He partially recovered but has been for many months very sick, his disease having been induced by his exposure in the service.

George R. Hanson, 27. Reg. (See page 128), was one of the Band of this Reg. that accompanied it to North Carolina under Gen. Burnside. Mr. Hanson was at the capture of Roanoke Island and Newbern and in various expeditions in North Carolina, but the Government having issued an order for the discontinuance of Regimental Bands he was discharged Aug. 31. 1862 and came home. At a later period he reentered the service in the 2d Heavy Artillery in which he remained for two years, doing garrison duty in N. Carolina; was Corporal and Sergeant in it; and July 3. 1865 was commissioned First

Lieutenant in the 14. U. S. Colored Heavy Artillery and Nov. 16. 1865 was commissioned as Captain in the same. Mr. Hanson was discharged Dec. 11. 1865.

James Harkins Jr., 31. Reg. (See page 129), was first in the service as a member of the 1st New York Mounted Riflemen, and served in Virginia and North Carolina. In the latter State he was captured and taken to Petersburg and to Richmond but after about five months he was exchanged and his time of service having expired he was discharged. Jan. 1. 1864 he reentered the service joining the 31. Reg. of Mass. Volunteers, but was at once transferred to the 6th Mass. Cavalry and went with Gen. Banks on the Red River Expedition. In the engagement at Alexandria La. he very narrowly escaped death or capture, his horse having been repeatedly shot under him. Not long after this he was in another desperate conflict when he was again taken prisoner and carried to Tyler Texas. After some time, an opportunity presenting itself he escaped and made his way back through swamps and thickets to Louisiana and reached Morganza 400 miles from Taylor in 27 days arriving Aug. 15. 1864, but he was soon taken sick with rheumatic fever and after being removed to New Orleans died Aug. 30. 1864.

Edwin C. Hastings, 6. Battery (See page 137), went to New Orleans but had been in service only a short time before an Artillery Box fell upon his back injuring him severely.   In a fainting fit he fell near the Hospital and lay upon the ground for some time during a storm which greatly aggravated his injury.   After he was able to walk he came home on a furlough in the spring of 1864 and went into the Hospital at Readville Mass.   April 1865 he was transferred to the Dale Hospital at Worcester where he remained till he was discharged May 26. 1865. Mr. Hastings has been a great sufferer, and his injury will be a permanent one, but he is gradually improving in health.

William Hill, 27. Reg. (See page 127), went with his Reg. to North Carolina but in the engagement at Roanoke Island Feb. 8. 1862 he was mortally wounded by a ball that passed through him and lodged in his overcoat, and died two days after.   Mr. Hill was buried at Roanoke Island and left two sons in the service and two daughters in Athol.   He was the first man from Athol who was killed in the war.

Charles H. Hill, 2d Reg. (See page 122), son of the above William Hill, was among the first that went into the service from Athol and was with his Reg. in the various engagements under Gen. Banks in the Shenandoah ·Valley. He was also in the battles at Antietam, Fredericksburg, Chancellorsville and Gettysburg Pa. In the last mentioned engagement he was wounded in the leg and after the ball was extracted he was in Hospitals at York Pa. Philadelphia and Portsmouth Grove R. I. Recovering near the close of 1863 Mr. Hill rejoined his Reg. and remained with it till the term of his enlistment had expired when he was discharged and came home, being the first man to return to Athol after three years service.

Andrew J. Hill, 21. Reg. (See page 125), son of William Hill and brother of Charles H. Hill above ; went with his Reg. into service in North Carolina and was in the engagement at the capture of Roanoke Island. While standing in the water during that battle he took a severe cold which brought on a fever and he died at Roanoke Island March 3. 1862. Mr. Hill was buried there, but high water prevented his comrades from laying his remains by the side of those of his father.

Samuel A. Hill, 21. Reg. (See page 125), was made corporal and went with his Reg. to North Carolina, was in the engagements at Ro-

anoke Island and in the thickest of the strife at
Newbern. In the battle at Camden N. C. four
balls passed through his overcoat but he escaped unhurt. In the summer of 1862 the
health of Mr. Hill failed and after a service of
thirteen months he was discharged and came
home. The date of his discharge is Oct. 31.
1862.

James S. Hodge, 27. Reg. (See page 127),
was Drummer and went with his Company to N.
Carolina; was at his post during the engagements at Roanoke Island, Newbern, Kinston,
Whitehall, Goldsboro' Washington and Gum
Swamp, received a furlough to visit his family
in Athol but while passing through Springfield
on his way home he was killed by the cars, Sept.
20. 1863. His funeral was attended in Athol
Sept. 22. 1863.

Aaron H. Holt, 53. Reg. (See page 132),
went with his Reg. to Louisiana and was with
his Company during all its engagements and
marches in that State and Mississippi, including
the capture of Fort Bisland and Port Hudson,
and returned with his Reg. to Massachusetts
Aug. 24. 1863, in health.

Lovell H. Horton, 27. Reg. (See page 126),

was commissioned 2d Lieutenant of Comp. B at the time of its organization, went with his Reg. to North Carolina but in the first engagement, viz. that at Roanoke Island he was injured by the explosion of a shell near him, though not wounded. Mr. Horton resigned his commission and was discharged Feb. 22. 1862 and returned home.

Albert Horton, 11th U. S. Infantry (See page 135), was Drummer and went into the service in the Summer of 1861 — and in all his early engagements acted as Orderly for the Surgeon; was at his post of duty in the battles at Gains' Mills, Malvern Hill, White Oak Swamp, 2d Bull Run, South Mountain, Antietam, Fredericksburg, Chancellorsville and Gettysburg. When Mr. Horton had been nearly two years in the service he was transferred to the Regimental Band for good conduct and continued in it till his term of enlistment had expired. Nov. 16. 1864 he re-entered the service in the same Reg. was with it in its various conflicts as the war was brought to its close, and is still with it in Virginia, having served at this time four years and two months.

Gardner Howe, 32. Reg. (See page 130), was at Fort Warren and went with his Reg. to Washington and Harrison's Landing Va., was

with his Reg. in the 2d Bull Run fight and when
the invading rebel army was driven out of Maryland; was in the desperate battle at Fredericksburg near the close of 1862 and was injured
while helping to carry a wounded man from the
field; was injured still more the next day while
carrying back the dead body of his Captain
Dearborn who had fallen at the front; went into
the Hospital, but his disease (inflammation of the
bowels) continuing, he was discharged March 7.
1863 and returned home very feeble. In Aug.
1864 Mr. Howe reentered the service in the 9.
Reg. Veteran Reserve Corps in which he did
duty till Sept. 8. 1865, when his health failing
again he was discharged and returned home, unable to labor. His second service was credited
to the town of Templeton.

John W. Howe, 27. Reg. (See page 127), was
among the recruits from Athol that joined the Reg.
early in 1864 and was with it in its first engagements of that year in Virginia; was at Port
Walthall, Arrowfield Church and Drury's Bluff;
was taken prisoner at the last mentioned place,
and carried to Richmond thence to Danville and
thence to Andersonville Ga., where he died of
Chronic Diarrhœa July 24. 1864. His disease
was doubtless the result of cruel treatment.
Mr. Howe left a wife in Athol. The No. of Mr.
Howe's grave is 3871.

George H. Hoyt, 1st Kansas Cavalry (See page 137), enlisted early in 1861 in John Brown Jr's Company of Sharp shooters and after becoming connected with the 1. Kansas Cav. was Commissioned 2d Lieutenant. Early in 1862 Mr Hoyt was made Captain in that Reg. and served as such under Generals Grant and Rosecrans in West Kentucky, Tennessee and Mississippi. Resigning on account of sickness he returned to Kansas, but soon organized an independent body of men to protect the State against the savage Quantrell. After the sack of Lawrence Capt. Hoyt assisted to raise the 15. Kansas Cavalry and was made Lieut. Col. of that Regiment. This he led in the battles of Lexington, Little Blue, Independence, Big Blue, Byram's Ford, State Line, Westport, and Newtonia, and was a portion of the two years in this service in Command of 1. Brigade 1. Div. under Gen. Curtis. While Provost Marshal at Humboldt Tenn. in 1862, Capt. Hoyt issued a freedom Proclamation for his district which caused him to be relieved from holding that position, tho' his order was never revoked. Lieut. Col. Hoyt served till the Rebellion was crushed and adds at the close of a note to the Chairman of the Committee in charge of this Record, "neither of the Regiments with which I have been in service nor any of my men ever took prisoners or surrendered themselves."

17*

John Humphrey, of the Navy, (See page 135), joined the U. States Navy in the summer of 1861, went on board the receiving ship at Charlestown and afterwards was a marine on board the Cumberland when this ship was engaged in the capture of the Forts near Hatteras Inlet North Carolina Aug. 28. 1861.   Mr. Humphrey was also on board the Cumberland, when that ship with others was suddenly attacked by the rebel Ship Merrimac near Newport News Va. March 8. 1862, and was one of the six marines who were killed by a shot before the sinking of the Cumberland.   Mr. Humphrey's remains were not recovered but appropriate funeral services were held in the church of the First Cong. Society of Athol March 19. 1862.   A very large audience was present and Rev. Messrs Bailey, Norton and Fay of Athol and Rev. Mr. Nightingale of Groton participated in the services.

Horace Hunt, 2. Reg. (See page 122), was among the first men that enlisted from Athol and went with his Reg. to the Upper Potomac; was clerk for his Captain and afterwards in the Commissary Department; was with his Reg. in the advance and retreat of Gen. Banks in the Shenandoah Valley and other engagements in Virginia; went with it to New York to suppress riots and took a severe cold at that time, went with his Reg. to Tullahoma Tenn. where he was taken sick; was two weeks on his way home and returned very feeble; died at Athol April 7. 1864 and was buried from the Baptist Church April 10. his Pastor Rev. G. L. Hunt preaching a funeral discourse which was published. Mr. Hunt's disease was Consumption.

Joseph E. Jennings, 4. H. Artillery (See page 135), joined the Reg. and was with it doing garrison duty in the Forts near Washington during the whole period of his service, and was discharged July 17. 1865.

Milton N. Jillson, 27. Reg. (See page 127), joined his Reg. at the seat of war in North Carolina in the spring of 1862 and was with it in the engagements at Kinston, Whitehall, Goldsboro', Washington and Gum Swamp N. C. and at Port Walthall and Arrowfield Church Va.; was severely wounded in the right shoulder May 14. 1864, from which wound he has continued to suffer more or less; partially recovering he returned to his Reg. and was detailed for Hospital duty when the Yellow Fever was prevailing at Newbern, had the Fever but recovered and was at length discharged at the expiration of the term of his enlistment May 1. 1865, returning home in comfortable health.

William H. Johnson, 21. Reg. (See page 125), went with this Reg. to Annapolis and North Carolina, was in the engagements at Roanoke Island and Newbern in the latter of which he fell mortally wounded and died the next day March 15. 1862. IIis remains were buried with those of a number of his comrades at Newbern.

Alfred Johnson, 13. Reg. (See page 124), was with his Reg. in the engagements at Cedar Mountain, Thoroughfare Gap, Bull Run No. 2, South Mountain, Antietam (where he was slightly wounded) Fredericksburg, Chancellorsville and Gettysburg where he was taken prisoner. Being paroled for exchange he returned home, but went back to his Reg. and served for the period of three years.

Thomas Johnson, 2. Reg. (See page 122), was among the first to go into service from Athol, and was with his Reg. in all the engagements in the Shenandoah Valley, in Tennessee and Georgia; reenlisted Jan. 1864 and was with Gen. Sherman in his triumphant march through Georgia and the Carolinas, but when his Reg. reached Washington in the summer of 1865, under the mistaken opinion that the veterans were to be retained in service while the new troops were mustered out, he deserted. His service in all other respects was honorable.

William A. Judd, 53. Reg. (See page 132), went with his Reg. to Louisiana and was detailed as Nurse in the Hospital March 1. 1863; was in the same capacity at Baton Rouge a month later and did not rejoin his Company till Aug. 9. Mr. Judd returned home with his Reg. Aug. 24. 1863.

Arthur N. Judd, 53. Reg. (See page 132), brother of the above, went with his Reg. to Louisiana but was carried to the Marine Hospital at New Orleans sick with Rheumatism Feb. 3. 1863; was taken prisoner at Brashear City June 23, was carried to Ship Island and exchanged July 9. returned to N. Orleans Aug. 5. rejoined his Company Aug. 11. and returned with it Aug. 24. 1863. In 1864 Mr. Judd reentered the service in the 29. Unattached Company Heavy Artillery and did garrison duty in the Forts near Washington till the close of the war, when he returned to Athol. His discharge was July 16. 1865.

James Kelley, 27. Reg. (See page 122), went with the Reg. to Annapolis where he was detailed Orderly for Gen. Foster and served in this capacity in the battles at Roanoke Island and Newbern, and in various other marches and engagements in North Carolina; went with Gen. Foster to Tennessee when that General relieved Gen. Burnside and was with him as Orderly till the

three years of his enlistment had expired. Mr.
Kelley was discharged Oct. 1. 1864 and returned
to Athol.

George L. Kendall, 27. Reg. (See page 127),
was one of the recruits that joined the Reg. in
North Carolina in 1862: was soon detailed Orderly for Col. Lee of the 27. Reg. and served in
this capacity in various expeditions and engagement in North Carolina and Virginia, particularly in the siege of Washington, at Gum Swamp,
at Walthall, Arrowfield Church and Drury's Bluff.
After the capture of Col. Lee Mr. Kendall was
again detailed to serve in the Quartermaster's
Department, and was discharged at the close of
the period of his enlistment, Sept. 27. 1864.

Charles L. Kendall, 99. N. Y. Reg. (See page
136), enlisted as a Musician in this Reg. when it
was known as " the Coast Guard " and served at
Fortress Monroe till the close of the Summer of
1862 when by a Government order the Regimental Bands were discontinued. Mr. Kendall's
second enlistment was in 1863 in the Band of
the 1st Brigade 2d Division 6th Corps and he
served at the Wilderness, Spottsylvania, North
Anna, Coal Harbor, Petersburg, Winchester,
Fisher's Hill, Middletown and other places till
the war closed and he was discharged. He en-

tered the service the third time in the Band of
the School Ship, stationed at New London Ct.
and is now (Jan. 1866) doing duty at that post.

Charles W. Kendall, 53. Reg. (See page 132),
was made Corporal Oct. 17. 1862, went with his
Reg. to Louisiana and April 8. 1863 was detailed
as Harness Maker in the Quartermaster's Department, and by virtue of this detail returned to
the ranks; rejoined the Company Aug. 11. and
returned home with it Aug. 24. 1863.

C. Dwight Kelton, 32. Reg. (See page 130),
joined the Reg. at Fort Warren and went with it
to Washington and Harrison's Landing Va. accompanied it to Maryland when the rebels invaded that State; was detailed to care for a sun
struck comrade F. W. Ripley, whom he took to
the house of a Mr. Smizer, Silver Springs, Md.;
remained there till the sick man was better, when
he went to Alexandria Va. on his return to his
Reg., was taken sick at that place of Pneumonia
and died there Oct. 31. 1862. His Father Calvin
Kelton Esqr. had his remains disinterred and
brought to Athol for final burial, and the funeral
was in the church of the Evangelical Society of
Athol Nov. 11. 1862. Inquiries directed to Silver Springs brought an interesting account of
his watching and labors there, and the day be-

fore his burial a letter came from Mr. Ripley to
C. Kelton Esqr. making inquiries after his son
and acknowledging his faithful service as the ap-
parent means of saving the life of his comrade.

Thomas Kenney, 27. Reg. (See page 128), was
one of the Band that accompanied the 27. Reg.
to North Carolina; and after serving at Roanoke
Island, Newbern and in various expeditions was
discharged Aug. 30. 1862 by a Government Order discontinuing Regimental Bands.

Owen Kenney, 21 Reg. (See page 125), broth-
or of the above, went with his Reg. into service
in North Carolina and was in the engagements
at Roanoke Island and Newbern. At a later
period he entered the 2d U. S. Cavalry, and is
supposed to have served in it till the three years
of his enlistment had expired.

Joseph W. Kilburn, 2. Vermont Reg. (See page
136), enlisted as early as May 1861 and was in
Washington with his Reg. June 20.; was in the
1st Bull Run battle and afterwards in the engagements at Lee's Mills, Williamsburg, and in
the seven days fight near Richmond, at Antietam, at Fredericksburg in both battles, at Banks
Ford, at Gettysburg, at Rappahannock Station
and in the first of the severe engagements under

Gen. Grant commencing May 5. 1864. Mr. Kilburn was run over while on duty, May 12. by a mounted aid and severely injured in the back, but had been in the Hospital only a single month when the three years of his enlistment expired and he was discharged June 29. 1864. Mr. Kilburn has nearly recovered from the injury received.

Lauriston I. King, 53 Reg. (See page 132), was left sick in the Hospital at New York when his Reg. went to Louisiana; rejoined the Company March 5. 1863 but was left sick when Gen. Banks moved his troops April 9; remained feeble but during a part of the time performed light service in the Hospital; rejoined the Company Aug. 11. and returned with it very sick Aug. 24. failed rapidly late in Oct. and died Nov. 2. 1863 of a complication of diseases contracted in the service. His funeral was in the Church at So. Athol Nov. 4. 1864. Mr. King left a wife and one child.

Asa L. Kneeland, 32. Reg. (See page 130), went with the Reg. from Fort Warren to Washington and Harrison's Landing, and was in the battles at Antietam Md. and at Fredericksburg, Chancellorsville and other places in Va.; reenlisted Jan. 1864 and came home on a furlough,

18

had the Measles soon after his return to Va. which left him without the power of speech a number of weeks; was sent to one of the Hospitals at Washington when partially recovering he was made Steward of the Ward he had been in; was on duty there for nine days, when the rebel forces approached the Forts commanding Washington; returned to his Reg. Sept. 2. 1864 and was in some of the desperate charges on the rebel works at Petersburg; took part in the Weldon Rail Road Raid, and finally in all the great battles that resulted in the fall of Richmond and the surrender of Lee's Army, aided in receiving the arms of the rebel troops and then returned to Washington over the old battle fields to be present at the Grand Review and to be mustered out of service June 28. 1865 having served three years and seven months. Mr. Kneeland was commissioned 2d Lieut. in Comp. K. and 1st Lieut. in Company F.

Ebenezer Kneeland, 32. Reg. (See page 130), brother of the above; went with him and was in the battles at Antietam, Fredericksburg, Chancellorsville, Gettysburg, Williamsport, Manassas Gap &c. Reenlisted Jan. 1864 and came home on a furlough; returned and was in the battles at the Wilderness and Spottsylvania in the latter of which May 12. 1864 he was wound-

ed in the index finger of the left hand. This
wound proving very severe from inflammation
he came home to recruit and was transferred to
the Invalid Corps Dec. 26. 1864. Serving in
this Mr. Kneeland was a nurse in one of the
Hospitals at Washington, till he was finally discharged Aug. 11. 1865, and then returned home
in health.

C. Walter Knowlton, 32. Reg. (See page 130),
like his comrades mentioned above, went from
Fort Warren to Washington and into actual service in Virginia and Maryland, at Antietam,
Fredericksburg, Chancellorsville, Gettysburg,
Williamsport, Manassas Gap, Culpepper, Rappa-
pahannock Station, Mountain Run and Mine
Run; and in 1864 at the Wilderness, Spottsylvania, Shady Grove Church and before Petersburg.
In 1865 Mr. Knowlton participated in all the
battles near Richmond which resulted in its capture and after assisting to receive the rebel arms
at the surrender of Lee's army, he was mustered
out at Burksville Va. April 19. 1865, the three
years of his enlistment having expired.

Guilford W. Lamb, 16. Reg. (See page 124),
was among the number drafted from Athol July
1863 and was accepted and reported for service.
He joined his Reg. in Virginia and was in the

engagements at Mine Run, the Wilderness, Spottsylvania, Coal Harbor, before Petersburg, and others and having been discharged at the end of the war returned home.

Daniel W. Larned, 27. Reg. (See page 127), went with his Reg. into service in North Carolina; was 5th and afterwards Orderly Sergeant of Comp. B; was in the engagements at Roanoke Island, Newbern, Kinston, Whitehall, Goldsboro', the Siege of Washington and Gum Swamp; reenlisted Jan. 1864; was in the engagements at Port Walthall and Arrowfield Church in the latter of which he was severely wounded in the left foot, came home on a furlough and was disabled for seven months tho' for three months of this time he acted as Clerk of the Company. Dec. 3. 1864 he was commissioned 2d Lieutenant and March 8. 1865 he led the Company in the desperate fight near Kinston N. C. in which he was wounded in the right side and right leg and taken prisoner. Mr. Larned was carried first to Salisbury N. C. and thence to Libby Prison Richmond where he was very sick with a fever; but recovering was exchanged and rejoined his Reg. at Newbern and was mustered with his Reg. out of service June 26. 1865. Mr. Larned was made 1st Lieutenant April 6. 1865 and received a Captain's commission under the Governor's Order May 15. 1865.

Patrick Leonard, 21. Reg. (See page 125), went with his Reg. to North Carolina; was wounded very severely in the right leg in the battle of Roanoke Island and this wound proved fatal eight days after. Mr. Leonard died as the troops were leaving for the capture of Newbern and was buried on the Island.

Enoch T. Lewis, 53. Reg. (See page 133), was made Sergeant Oct. 17, 1862 and went with his Regiment to Louisiana; was in the fight at the capture of Fort Bisland, in all the marches of the Reg. and its engagements at the capture of Port Hudson and returned with his Reg. in health Aug. 24. 1863.

Elijah W. Lincoln, Navy. (See page 135), enlisted early in the war and went from Washington on board the Governor Steamer at Fortress Monroe as a marine, started for Hilton Head S. C. under Commodore Dupont; was shipwrecked off the coast of South Carolina; was one of 200 men who held up for 38 hours one of the large beams of the ship; was taken off at length in the night by the Sabine; went on to the coast of Florida, but was not engaged there; came back to Washington April 1862; went Nov. 1862 to Cairo and there remained on duty till the time of his enlistment had expired. Mr.

18*

Lincoln was made Corporal, then Sergeant and for eight months was Acting Lieutenant, and was discharged Aug. 19. 1865 with high commendations.

George W. Lincoln, 53. Reg. (See page 133), went with the 53. Reg. to Louisiana and was left sick at Algiers La. April 9. 1863 when Gen. Banks moved against the enemy and was not able to rejoin his Comp. till Aug. 11. He returned home in comfortable health Aug. 24. 1863. In 1864 Mr. Lincoln re-entered the service in the 5. Reg. under the call for one hundred days' men, but tho' he was anxious to go to the field and fell in three times when troops were sent forward he was nevertheless retained on service in the vicinity of Boston till the time of regular discharge, Nov. 16. 1864.

Fernaldo L. Lord, 27. Reg. (See page 127), was one of the recruits that joined the Reg. in North Carolina in 1862; was in the engagements at Kinston, Whitehall, Goldsboro', in the siege at Washington and at Gum Swamp; went with his Reg. to Va. and reenlisted Jan. 1864; came home and returned to take part in the battles at Port Walthall, Arrowfield Church, Coal Harbor and other places in Virginia; was with his Reg. in North Carolina early in 1865 and in the desperate conflict near Kinston March 8.; was severely wounded in the arm and taken prisoner with nearly every other man of his Reg.; was carried to Richmond and soon paroled for exchange, was sent to Annapolis, but his wound prevented him from active service till the time of his discharge, which was June 18. 1865. Mr. Lord was in service three years lacking one month.

Amos H. Locke, 99. N. Y. Reg. (See page 136), enlisted as Musician in this Reg. which was then known as "the Coast Guard" and stationed at Fortress Monroe, and did duty in the Band of it to which he belonged till Regimental Bands were discontinued by an order from the Government in 1862 when he returned home.

Martin L. Maynard, 36. Reg. (See page 131), went with his Reg. in 1862 into service in Va. was at the battle at Fredericksburg; accompanied his Reg. to Kentucky and when it protected the polls at Cincinnati, went with it into the engagements and shared in all its perils back of Vicksburg and returned with it to Kentucky and East Tennessee; helped to defend Knoxville but on one occasion, being lame, was obliged to throw away his musket and knapsack and run for his life; returned with the Reg. to

Virginia and was in the great battles before Petersburg-was invested; was terribly wounded in the leg there, the ball shattering the bones below the knee; had his limb amputated and was brought to the Dale Hospital at Worcester where he remained till he was discharged Feb. 5. 1865. Mr. Maynard is the only Athol soldier who lost a limb during the war.

John N. Mars, 1st North Carolina Reg. (See page 137). This was a Colored Reg. and Mr. Mars was commissioned as its Chaplain and joined it at Newbern; but being sick at the time the Reg. went to Folly Island during the attack on Charleston he did not accompany it. Remaining at Newbern some months in charge of Army Stores he was at length ordered to Norfolk and Portsmouth Va. where he remained as Chaplain for a number of Regiments till Jan. 1864. when his health having become impaired he asked for a discharge. This was at length granted him but he remained for some months in Va. laboring for the Freedmen, and is now, Jan. 1866, the honored pastor of a very large Colored Congregation in Baltimore.

Horatio W. McClellen, 27. Reg. (See page 127), was one of the recruits that joined this Reg. in North Carolina in 1862.; was in the

Kinston, Whitehall and Goldsboro' fights; participated in the defence of Washington N. C. and in the Gum Swamp engagement; was made Corporal June 19. 1863; was at Port Walthall and Arrowfield Church Va. in May 1864 and was wounded at the latter May 9. was removed to Philadelphia where he died of Scarletina June 21. 1864. leaving a mother in Athol.

Norris B. Meacham, 27. Reg. (See page 127), went to N. Carolina with his Reg. in 1861. was in the fights at Roanoke Island, Kinston, Whitehall and Goldsboro' also, in the siege of Washington and other engagements and expeditions in N. Carolina; was at Port Walthall, Arrowfield Church and Drury's Bluff. Va. in 1864. was captured with 29 others of his Company in the fight last mentioned; was in Libby Prison one week and in Andersonville four months where he suffered greatly from starvation and scurvy; was taken to Savannah and then to Millen Ga. and paroled Nov. 19. for exchange; was brought on to Annapolis very feeble, and reached home Jan. 24. 1864. Mr. Meacham gradually gained, but the term of his enlistment having expired long before, he was discharged March 7. 1865.

George W. Meacham, 27. Reg. (See page

127), was with his Reg. in the engagements at Roanoke Island and Newbern, but on the march to Trenton in July 1862 he was sunstruck and carried back to the Hospital. Oct. 16. 1862 he was discharged as unfit for duty and returned home.

In 1863 Mr. Meacham reentered the service in the 1st Heavy Artillery and went to the front with that Regiment. In the battle at Spottsylvania May 19. 1864 this Reg. lost very heavily and Mr. Meacham had a finger shot off and was also slightly wounded in the hip. He was sent to one of the Hospitals in Philadelphia, where after his recovery, he was employed as a nurse till the end of the war and was discharged May 16. 1865.

Isaiah S. Merrill, 61. Reg. (See page 137), left with his Reg. for Fortress Monroe in Oct. 1864 and went to City Point where the Reg. was put into the Engineer Brigade and worked six months on the defences of City Point. April 2. 1865 Mr. Merrill was in the great charge upon the Forts before Petersburg and entered that city with his Reg. the next day ; went to Burksville April 18. and a few days later started for Washington, through Richmond. On a review in that city Mr. Merrill was partially sunstruck, and a few days later was struck down in the

same manner and left on the ground as the Reg.
moved on and so was obliged with a single comrade to walk to Washington which city he
reached May 13. June 3. 1865 Mr. Merrill was
mustered out of service with his Reg. and returned home in comfortable health. He was
counted upon the quota for North Adams.

John F. Merrill, 10. Reg. (See page 123), brother of the above, went into the service when
this Reg. was formed in 1861, and accompanied
it to Washington and at a later period to the
front in Virginia; took part in the operations at
Yorktown and Williamsburg and in the battle
of May 8. 1862 at Savage's Station and June 25.
at Fair Oaks was severely wounded by a ball
that entered the upper part of his chest and
passing through his lungs was cut out in his
back. He began to bleed profusely but was
carried from the field by his brother James L.
Merrill, and supported by him in a sitting pos-
ture for much of the time for five weeks to prevent hemorrhage when he began to gain tho' he
could not lie down for three months without
internal bleeding; was at length removed to a
Hospital at Baltimore where he remained about
five months before he could come home. Mr.
Merrill was discharged Sept. 15. 1862 and has
gradually improved in health, tho' he may never

be well.   IIe has repeatedly tried to reenter the
service but could not be accepted.   The part of
his overcoat carried into the wound in his chest
passed through his lungs and was taken out,
months after the ball, from the opening in his
back.

James L. Merrill, 10. Reg. (See page 123),
brother of the above; went like him into service
in Washington and Virginia; was with his brother at Yorktown, Williamsburg, Savage's Station
and Fair Oaks, had the lock of his musket carried away just as his brother fell as detailed
above; was ordered by his Captain Miller to
care for his wounded brother which he did went
with him to Baltimore, where he himself was sick
for many months, tho' he acted as nurse a part
of the time in the Hospital; and at the end of
sixteen months in the Hospital, viz. Aug. 28.
1863 he was discharged as unable to continue in
the service.   Mr. Merrill has in a good degree
regained his health.

Joseph A. Merrill, 36. Reg. (See page 131),
brother of the above; went with his Reg. to
Washington and into service in Va. was first in
battle at Fredericksburg, and then went with his
Reg. to Kentucky and was in the chase after the
rebel Gen. Morgan; went to Mississippi and was

in the engagements back of Vicksburg till its capture; returned to Kentucky and went into East Tennessee; was in the battle of Blue Springs and helped defend Fort Saunders near Knoxville; returned to Va. in March 1864 and was in the battles of the Wilderness, Spottsylvania, Coal Harbor and before Petersburg, June 17. 1864. July 28. Mr Merrill was severely wounded in the head by a ball, just as he had raised his rifle to fire, and was helped off the field by his brother Henry, named below, and another comrade. Partially recovering, he came home, but the injury received rendered him unfit for longer service and he was discharged Dec. 19. 1864. Up to this time Jan. 1866, his health has not been restored. Mr. Merrill was made Sergeant July 1. 1863.

Henry S. Merrill, 36. Reg. (See page 131), brother of the four mentioned above, was like his brother Joseph A. in the engagement at Fredericksburg, and in service in Kentucky and back of Vicksburg; was very sick while his Reg. was in service in East Tennessee, but was with it in the battle of the Wilderness May 6. 1864 and was severely wounded there by a ball that penetrated his side; was among the 280 wounded soldiers who fought their way back to Fredericksburg, still carrying his rifle, crossed the river and at length reached Acquia Creek; helped construct a raft and was taken off from it in the Potomac; was carried to Washington where the ball was at length extracted and he came home on a furlough. Six other balls passed through his coat &c. in the encounter. Partially recovering, Mr. Merrill rejoined his Reg. and was with it in all the desperate fighting that resulted in the fall of Richmond and the overthrow of the Confederacy, and was discharged with his Reg. June 8. 1865, having previously received a second shot in his neck, which appears to have given him but little concern.

Jonathan B. Mills, 36. Reg. (See page 131), went with his Reg. to Washington and was engaged with it at Fredericksburg, in Kentucky and back of Vicksburg; was sun struck the day the Reg. left for Kentucky and was left behind; overtook the Reg. in Kentucky and went with it into the hard service in East Tennessee when the men were glad to pick up and eat the kernels of corn found in the streets; was sick on the return of the Reg. to Maryland and was four weeks in the Hospital at Annapolis his disease being Hernia, and the feebleness induced by this added to his deafness which at that time rendered him unfit for service procured for him his discharge Dec. 10. 1864. Mr. Mills's health is in a good degree restored.

Edmund Moore, 27. Reg. (See page 127), went with his Reg. to Annapolis and North Carolina; was soon detailed as Orderly for Capt. Fearing on Gen. Burnside's Staff, and served in this capacity wherever Gen. Burnside had command, in North Carolina, Kentucky, Tennessee and Virginia, till the three years of his enlistment had expired. Mr. Moore was discharged Sept. 27. 1864 and returned home in health.

James A. Moore, 53. Reg. (See page 133), went with his Reg. into service in Louisiana was in the engagement at Fort Bisland, and participated in all the marches and expeditions of the Reg. up to June 14. 1863 when in the assault upon Port Hudson he was wounded in the head; was sent to the Hospital at Baton Rouge; rejoined the Reg. Aug. 5. and returned with it Aug. 24. 1863. Mr. Moore has continued to suffer from his wound, which seemed only slight at the first.

George F. Moore, 53. Reg. (See page 133), went with his Reg. to Louisiana and was with it, in health at Fort Bisland, Opelousas, Alexandria and Port Hudson doing his duty; was taken severely sick while the Reg. was returning home, and was left in the Hospital at Buffalo N. York. Mr. Moore soon recovered however and returned to Athol a few days after his comrades.

George McRae, 53. Reg. (See page 133), went with his Reg. to Louisiana and participated in the fighting at Fort Bisland and in the marches to Alexandria and back to the Mississippi; was taken sick before Port Hudson and sent into the Hospital at Baton Rouge but recovered sufficiently to rejoin his Company Aug. 9. and to return home with it Aug. 24. 1863.

John O. Mowry, 27. and 55. Reg. (See page 127), went with the 27. Reg. to North Carolina, and was in the engagements at Roanoke Island, Newbern, Kinston, Whitehall and Goldsboro', was also in the defence of Washington N. C. and in the battle of Gum Swamp, but in June 1863 he was transferred to the 55. Reg. (Colored) and made 2d Lieut. of Comp. I. July 10. 1863 Mr. Mowry was Commissioned 1st Lieut. of Comp. B. and went with the Reg. into service in South Carolina. He was on James Island in the fighting during the siege of Charleston and went with his Reg. to Florida under Gen. Seymour. He was also in the engagement at Honey Hill but was never sick severely, and was never wounded, during a service of three years and eleven and a half months. About fourteen months he was Quartermaster of his Reg. and as such he returned to Mass. with his Reg. and was mustered out of the service Sept. 22. 1865.

George Morse, 27. Reg. (See page 127), went with his Reg. to North Carolina but was sick during the engagements at Roanoke Island and Newbern and did not participate in either. Mr. Morse was Wagoner; but the state of his health was such that he was discharged April 4. 1862 and returned home, feeble, with his Brother Laban Morse Esqr. He has since regained his health in a good degree.

Henry T. Morse, 27. Reg. Band, (See page 128), went with his Reg. to North Carolina and in the battle at Roanoke Island aided in Hospital duties as stretcher bearer, but during the fight at Newbern was sick on board a transport; remained at Newbern on duty till Aug. 30. 1862 when the Reg. Bands having been discontinued by an order of Government, he returned home. Mr. Morse reentered the service in 1863 in the Band of the 1st Brigade, 2d Div. 6th Army Corps, and was three months at Harpers Ferry and afterwards in service in the battles of the Wilderness, Spottsylvania, No. Anna, Coal Harbor and before Petersburg; went to Washington when Gen. Early threatened that city and participated in his defeat and the pursuit of him: was then sick for a time but rejoined his Corps to be present in the battles of Winchester, Fisher's Hill and Middletown under Gen. Sheridan. Nov.

19*

11. 1864 at the consolidation of his Brigade he was discharged and returned home.

Leander B. Morse 27. and 56. Reg. (See page 128), brother of the above, went into service in North Carolina a member of the Band and after being on duty at Roanoke Island and Newbern was discharged Aug. 30. 1862 by a Government Order discontinuing the Regimental Bands. Mr. Morse reentered the service as a Musician in the 56. Reg. in 1863 and with his Reg. became a part of the Army of the Potomac; was on duty at the battles of the Wilderness, Spottsylvania, No. Anna, Coal Harbor, before Petersburg and at the Weldon Rail Road, and finally in the great movements of Gen. Grant in April 1865 which resulted in the fall of Richmond and the surrender of Gen. Lee's Army. Mr. Morse was mustered out of the service July 22. 1865 and returned home in health.

Frederick P. Morse, 56. Reg. (See page 134), served first for nine months in the 46. Reg. to fill the quota for Springfield. This part of his service was rendered in North Carolina. Mr. Morse reentered the service in 1863 and went with his Reg. the 56th to Virginia and was in the battles of the Wilderness, of Spottsylvania and in front of Petersburg, when his health failed and he returned to the Hospital at Readville Mass. where he remained for seven months. He rejoined his Reg. at Burkesville Va. returned with it to Alexandria and to Readville where he was discharged July 22. 1865.

John R. Morse, 27. Reg. (See page 127), brother of the above ; was made Corporal Oct. 1861 and went with his Reg. to N. Carolina ; was in the battles at Roanoke Island, Newbern, Kinston, Whitehall and Goldsboro' ; participated in the defence of Washington N. C. and in the engagement at Gum Swamp ; came with his Reg. to Virginia and was with it in all its expeditions and engagements up to the time when the three years of his enlistment expired, particularly at Port Walthall, Arrowfield Church, Drury's Bluff and Coal Harbor, escaping wounds and sickness. Mr. Morse was detailed for pioneer service which often made his exposure great. He was discharged Sept. 27. 1864.

George W. Nelson, 32. Reg. (See page 130), joined the Reg. when it was the First Battalion at Fort Warren ; went with it to Virginia ; was soon taken sick and was in the Hospital four months, disease Chronic Bronchitis ; was discharged Dec. 17. 1862 as unfit for service and returned home to regain his health.

John F. Nickerson, 11. U. S. Inf. (See page 135), was engaged in recruiting service the greater part of the time for eighteen months; was in the battle of Chancellorsville but soon after his health failed and he was transferred to the Invalid Corps. After having been in the service for about two years he was discharged Aug. 6. 1863.

Joseph Nickerson, 11. U. S. Inf. (See page 135), brother of the above, was engaged like his brother in recruiting for one year ; was in the battles at Antietam, Sharpsburg, Fredericksburg, Chancellorsville and Gettysburg, was severely wounded in the last mentioned in his left arm, a ball passing through it ; recovering after two months he returned to his Reg. ; in the battle of the Wilderness he was taken prisoner, was carried to Richmond and thence to Andersonville and afterward to Savannah and Millen, was very much reduced by sickness and starvation and left his prison Nov. 7. with those who took the oath of Allegiance to the Confederacy ; did not take the oath but was prevented from escaping for a long time ; wandered over parts of Mississippi, Alabama, Georgia and South Carolina as a sick rebel soldier but could not reach the lines of the Union Army till after the occupation of Augusta Ga. by our troops, was then sent to Savannah and home receiving his discharge June 23. 1865. Mr. Nickerson was in the service three years and eleven months and a prisoner one year and six days.

Ruel R. Nickerson, 11. U. S. Inf. (See page 135), brother of the above — entered the service as a Drummer and was with his Reg. in the Peninsular Campaign under Gen. McClellan and in the battles of South Mountain and Antietam, but being disabled by a rupture he was discharged soon after the last mentioned engagements. Recovering, he enlisted in the Navy in the Autumn of 1864 and was on board the Gun Boat Talapoosa at and off Key West till the close of the war when he was discharged and returned in health. Mr. Nickerson was Hospital Steward on board the Talapoosa.

William Nute, 2. Reg. (See page 122), was in the Company of young men that first entered the service from Athol; was in the advance and retreat of Gen. Banks in the Shenandoah Valley and in the battle of Antietam, soon after which he was at his own request, transferred to the 4th U. S. Artillery, Comp. F which was called Bests' Battery. The transfer was made Oct. 1862. Mr. Nute served for three full years.

Adin Oakes, 53. Reg. (See page 133), went

with his Reg. to Louisiana and participated in
the Capture of Fort Bisland, in the marches to
and from Alexandria and in the first engagements at Port Hudson ; was wounded May 29.
1863 at the last mentioned place in his back and
was sent to the Hospital at Baton Rouge where
he died June 29. 1863 from the effects of his
wound.   Mr. Oakes was buried at Baton Rouge
and left a wife and children at Athol.

James Oliver Jr. 21. and 61. Reg. (See page
125), was commissioned, as soon as he had grad-
uated at the Medical College, Assistant Surgeon
in the 21. Reg. and joined that Reg. at Falmouth
Va.   In the 2d Bull Run which was his first engagement Dr. Oliver was left in charge of the
sick and wounded and taken prisoner, but soon
managed to escape.   He rejoined his Reg. at
Alexandria and participated in the battles at
South Mountain and Antietam and Oct. 11. 1862
was ordered to Locust Spring Hospital at Antietam, where were four hundred badly wounded to
be taken to Frederick City Md.   Rejoining his
Reg. Feb. 1863 he went with it through Kentucky and Cumberland Gap into East Tennessee
to participate in the battles of Blue Springs,
London and the famous defence of Knoxville.
Jan. 1864 Dr. Oliver re-enlisted and took the
sick and wounded by the way of Chattanooga

and Nashville to Cincinnati while his Reg. marched over the mountains. Dr. Oliver was now Surgeon of the 21. Reg. and as such in 1864 he passed through the battles of the Wilderness, Spottsylvania, Bethesda Church, Coal Harbor, the advance on Petersburg, the night charge of June 17. and the blowing up of the Burnside Mine July 30. He was promoted Surgeon May 26. 1864, and having served three years was mustered out, Aug. 30. In Sept. 1864 he was commissioned Assistant Surgeon of the 61. Reg.; Oct. 18. Surgeon of the same and June 2. 1865 Brigade Surgeon — and participated in the great battles of April 1865 which resulted in the fall of Richmond and the overthrow of the Rebellion. From Burkesville Va., Dr. Oliver came on through Richmond to Washington and was mustered out with his Reg. July 30. 1865.

James Oliver, 2d, 27. Reg. (See page 127), was among the recruits that joined his Reg. in N. Carolina in 1862; participated in the engagements at Kinston, Whitehall and Goldsboro', also in the defence of Washington N. C. and at Gum Swamp. In Dec. 1863 Mr. Oliver was detailed as Regimental Armorer at Norfolk Va. which accounts for his escape from capture at Drury's Bluff. Soon after the battle of Coal Harbor he was sick two weeks; then he was detailed in the

Hospital as nurse and then as Carpenter at the Base Hospital near the Point of Rocks on the Appomattox River; then left the front, the time of his enlistment having expired and was discharged, in health, Sept. 27. 1864.

Aaron Oliver, 27. Reg. (See page 127), was among the recruits who joined this Reg. in 1864; participated in ths expedition to Suffolk and was at Port Walthall and Arrowfield Church, was at the Camp in the rear during the fight at Drury's Bluff, and after being in other engagements, was taken prisoner March 8. 1865 near Kinston N. C. was carried to Richmond and soon paroled for exchange, and was discharged with his Reg. June 22. 1865.

Sylvanus E. Oliver, 27. Reg. (See page 127), went with his Reg. to North Carolina in 1862 and participated in the engagements at Roanoke Island, Newbern, Kinston, Whitehall, Goldsboro', in the defence of Washington and at Gum Swamp; was afterwards at Arrowfield Church and in the desperate battle of Drury's Bluff May 16. 1864 where he was taken prisoner with 247 others of his Reg. was carried to Libby Prison Richmond, thence to Danville, and thence to Andersonville Ga. where he died of Chronic Diarrhœa brought on by starvation and cruel treatment Aug. 14. 1864. When carried to the prison Hospital Mr. Oliver was too low to recognize his comrades. The No. of his grave is 4640.

Otis Oliver, 27. Reg. (See page 127), brother of the above, went with his Reg. to North Carolina and participated in the battles of Roanoke Island and Newbern, in the latter of which he was wounded in the knee, from which he has never wholly recovered, but rejoined his Reg. and was in the engagements at Kinston, Whitehall and Goldsboro' and in the siege of Washington N. C. and at Gum Swamp; was transferred Aug. 4. 1863 to the Invalid Corps, and sent to New York — and to Washington when that city was threatened by Gen. Early, and finally discharged Oct. 3. 1864.

Franklin Oliver, Jr., 27. Reg. (See page 127), brother of the above; went like his brothers Sylvanus and Otis with his Reg. to North Carolina; was in the engagements at Roanoke Island and at Newbern in the latter of which he was wounded in the back by a spent ball, but recovered in season to be with his Reg. at Kinston, Whitehall, Goldsboro' and its other engagements and marches in North Carolina and Virginia, escaped capture at Drury's Bluff, and was dis-

20

charged in health at the close of three years' service viz. Sept. 27. 1864 and returned home.

Ozi Oliver, 53. Reg. (See page 133), the last of four brothers that entered the service; went with his Reg. to Louisiana and was engaged at Fort Bisland, participated in all the tedious marches of the Reg. and in the fights before Port Hudson and returned with his Reg. in health Aug. 24. 1863.

Ansel Orcott, 21. Reg. (See page 125), went with his Reg. to Annapolis and into service in North Carolina; was in the engagements at Roanoke Island and Newbern, in the latter of which he was slightly wounded and had his musket struck in each engagement; is supposed to have been in other engagements the particulars of which cannot be learned and to have been discharged at the close of three years' service. Mr. Orcott was for some months in the Hospital at Portsmouth Grove R. I.

J. Henry Packard, 27. Reg. (See page 127), went with his Reg. to North Carolina and was in the battles at Roanoke Island, Newbern, Kinston, Whitehall, Goldsboro', in and about Washington N. C. and at Gum Swamp. Mr. Packard was in the Hospital at Portsmouth Va. during the campaign of the 27. Reg. in that State, sick with Rheumatism but recovered and at the close of the three years of his enlistment, was discharged, viz. Sept. 27. 1864. Mr. Packard was for a considerable time Cook for his Company.

James C. Parker, 21. Reg. (See page 125), went with his Reg. to Annapolis and was Cook for his Company; went in this capacity to North Carolina; was sick at the time of the capture of Roanoke Island and on board a transport; was mortally wounded by a ball through the abdomen in the battle of Newbern and died the next day March 15. 1862. Mr. Parker was in the thickest of the fight, but his rifle missed fire each time. He was buried at Newbern and left in Athol a wife (since dead) and three children.

Chauncey Parkman Jr., 1. H. Artillery, (See page 134), went to his Reg. into service in Virginia and was in the battle at Spottsylvania May 17. 1864 when he was severely and as it proved fatally wounded by a shell in the head and side; was removed with the wounded to Harewood Hospital Washington where he died June 3. 1864. Mr. Parkman left one child in Athol. He was buried at Washington.

Emory A. Peckham, 27. Reg. (See page 127),

went with the 27th to North Carolina and participated in the engagements at Roanoke Island,
Newbern, Kinston, Whitehall and Goldsboro',
also in the defence of Washington N. C. and in
the battle of Gum Swamp.   Mr. Peckham accompanied his Reg. to Virginia when it engaged
the enemy at Port Walthall, Arrowfield Church,
Coal Harbor and other places, and having served
three years was discharged Sept. 27. 1864 and
returned home in health.

Freeman G. Perry, 53. Reg. (See page 133),
went with his Reg. to Louisiana and after being
in the engagement at Fort Bisland and participating in the marches of the 53d to Alexandria
and back to the Mississippi River at Port Hudson he was taken sick and sent to the Hospital
at Baton Rouge June 5. 1863.   Mr. Perry rejoined the Company of Capt. Fay, July 14. and
returned with it to Athol Aug. 24. 1863.   May
1. 1863 Mr. Perry was made Corporal in Comp.
E in the place of C. W. Kendall, detailed as
Harness Maker.

Leander W. Phelps, 2. Reg. (See page 123),
and 1. Heavy Artillery (See page 134), was the
first man that offered himself as a soldier in
Athol at the breaking out of the Rebellion ;
was mustered into the service May 11. 1861,

and went with the first company of soldiers from this place under Col. Gordon to the Upper Potomac; was in the engagements at and about Winchester Va. during Gen. Banks's advance and retreat in the Shenandoah Valley when our troops were ten days without rations; was slightly wounded in the hip at the 1st Fredericksburg battle; was in the engagements at Cedar Mountain and Antietam, in the last of which he was severely wounded by a ball which passed through his hand. Being disabled he was discharged April 3. 1863, but recovering the use of his hand he reentered the service in the 1st Heavy Artillery and was engaged in the battles at Spottsylvania Court House, No. Anna River, Tolopotomy Creek, Coal Harbor, Petersburg in June 1864, Strawberry Plains, Deep Bottom, Poplar Spring Church, Boydton Plank Road, Weldon Rail Road, Hatcher's Run and finally participated in the conflicts of April 1865 when Lee's army was routed and Petersburg and Richmond captured, soon after which he was discharged and returned to Athol with health impaired. Mr. Phelps was first Corporal of his Company.

Foster W. Phelps, 27. Reg. (See page 128), went with his Reg. to Annapolis and into service in North Carolina and was detailed as Orderly for Gen. Foster; served with him in this capacity during the Campaigns in North Carolina, Kentucky and Tennessee; reenlisted in 1864 and was immediately detached from his Company for the same service with Gen. Foster; was sick at home for the period of eight months after reenlisting and was discharged at the close of the war, viz. June 12. 1865, having served three years and nine months.

Charles C. Phelps, 21. Reg. (See page 125), brother of the above mentioned Leander and Foster, went with the Reg. to North Carolina and was detailed as private Orderly for Major Richmond; served in this capacity for two months when he held the same position under Maj. Gen. Burnside, and was with him in all his battles and marches in North Carolina, Virginia, Kentucky and Tennessee. Mr. Phelps reenlisted Feb. 12. 1864 and was at once detached from the 21. Reg. for his service under Gen. Burnside, and when that General resigned Mr. Phelps was ordered to report to Maj. Gen. Park. He was discharged July 22. 1865 and returned to Athol in health.

Asa Philips, 30. Reg. (See page 129), went with the Reg. into camp at Pittsfield and started for the seat of war under Gen. Butler, but died at or near Fortress Monroe Jan. 30. 1862. His remains were brought to Athol for burial and he left here a wife and children.

John R. Pierce, 53. Reg. (See page 133), though not subject to a draft, enlisted and went with his Regiment to Louisiana, was detailed as Chief Cook of Comp. E Oct. 17. 1862; went with his Reg. on all its expeditions and was with it in all its engagements up to July 4. 1863 when he was sent from before Port Hudson and just before its capture to the Hospital at Baton Rouge, sick; started for Mass. on board the St. Mary's Aug. 7. arrived in New York Aug. 14. and reached home Aug. 19. 1863, very feeble but improving. Mr. Pierce regained his health.

Albert D. Pond, 27. Reg. (See page 128), went with his Reg. into service in North Carolina and was with it in the engagements at Roanoke Island, Newbern, Kinston, Whitehall and Goldsboro'; was on duty constantly in the defence of Washington N. C. and was engaged at Gum Swamp; went with the Reg to Virginia, reenlisted Jan. 1864, and after a furlough of thirty days returned to take part in the engagements at Port Walthall, Arrowfield Church, Drury's Bluff (where he escaped capture), Coal Harbor, and before Petersburg, was wounded June 3. in

the hip but disabled for a week only ; returned
with his Reg. to North Carolina and was Acting
Regimental Quartermaster at the time of the
desperate conflict near Kinston March 8. 1865
when nearly the entire Reg. was captured; was
discharged July 20. 1865 and returned home in
health.　Mr. Pond was made Corporal May 9.
1864, Sergeant Sept. 27. 1864 and was Commissioned First Lieutenant May 9. 1865.

John Plunkett, 30. Reg. (See page 129), joined
his Reg. in 1864 and was with it under Gen.
Sheridan in the last of the great battles in Virginia which resulted in the capture of Richmond
and Lee's Army and the overthrow of the Confederacy.　Mr. Plunkett is at this time, Jan.
1866, still in service with his Reg. in Virginia.

Rufus Putnam 53. Reg. (See page 133), was
detailed for Hospital service Oct. 17. 1862 ; was
left as Nurse in the Hospital at Baton Rouge
April 1. 1863 ; served in this capacity till Aug. 9.
1863 when he rejoined the Company and returned with it to Athol in health Aug. 24. 1863.

John E. Rand, 21. and 56. Reg. (See page 125),
went into service with the 21. Reg. in North Carolina; was in the battles at Roanoke Island,
Newbern and Camden, in the last of which he

was wounded in the hand and slightly in the abdomen, (a ball striking a button and glancing apparently prevented the latter from being a fatal wound.) Mr. Rand was also in the 2d Bull Run fight when he was taken prisoner but was paroled for exchange the next day, but having been partially disabled he was discharged Jan. 25. 1863. A few months later he reentered the service in the 56th Reg. but whether he served in it or not, those in charge of this record are uncertain.

Joshua Rich, 32. Reg. (See page 131), went with this Reg. into service in Va. and with it to Lexington Kentucky and to protect the polls at Cincinnati Ohio; accompanied the Reg. to Mississippi and was in the engagement at Jackson and in all the service in the rear of Vicksburg; returned to Kentucky and assisted in the defence of Knoxville in East Tennessee; came to Virginia and was killed in the battle of the Wilderness May 6. 1864. A ball passed through the body of Mr. Rich from side to side and he lived but three hours after he was wounded, his remains falling into the hands of the enemy. Mr. Rich was made Corporal April 1. 1863. He left a wife in Athol.

Samuel Rich, 27. Reg. (See page 128), was

with his Reg. nearly three years in service in North Carolina and Virginia, participating in the engagements at Roanoke Island, Newbern, Kinston, Whitehall, Goldsboro', the defence of Washington N. C. and at Gum Swamp, as also in the expedition to Suffolk Va. and in the battles at Port Walthall, Arrowfield Church and Drury's Bluff, in the last mentioned of which he was taken prisoner with a large number of his comrades; was taken to Richmond, thence to Danville and then to Andersonville Ga., where he died of Chronic Diarrhœa induced by starvation and cruel treatment, July 28. or Aug. 1. 1864. The number of his grave is 4233.

William Richardson, 27. Reg. (See page 128), also of the 56. Reg. (See page 134), belonged to the Band of the 27. Reg. and went with it into service in North Carolina; was on duty at Roanoke Island and in the capture of Newbern, but was discharged Aug. 31. 1862 by a Government Order discontinuing Regimental Bands. Mr. Richardson returned to Athol but reentered the service in 1863 as a Musician in the 56. Reg. and went with this Reg. when it became a part of the Army of the Potomac under Gen. Grant; served in the battles of the Wilderness, Spottsylvania, No. Anna, Coal Harbor, before Petersburg and at the Weldon Rail Road; and finally participated in the capture of Richmond, Petersburg and Lee's Army and the overthrow of the Confederacy. Mr. Richardson was discharged July 22. 1865 and returned home in health.

James H. Richardson, 27. Reg. (See page 128), participated in the engagements of his Reg. in North Carolina and Virginia up to May 16. 1864, particularly in the capture of Roanoke Island and Newbern, and in the engagements at Kinston, Whitehall, Goldsboro', in and about Washington N. C. and at Gum Swamp; also at Port Walthall, Arrowfield Church and Drury's Bluff Va.; was taken prisoner at Drury's Bluff May 16. 1864; was carried to Richmond, to Danville and to Andersonville Ga., was also in the rebel prisons at Savannah and Millen Ga.; was brought very low by starvation and disease but in Nov. 1864 was paroled for exchange and brought to Annapolis; came home early in Jan. 1865 very feeble but improving and was discharged Jan. 18. of the same year. Mr. Richardson, like many others, barely escaped with his life, but has completely recovered.

Delavan Richardson, 2. Reg. (See page 123), went with the first Company of soldiers from Athol soon after the breaking out of the Rebellion and was in all the engagements of the 2d

Reg. in Virginia, Maryland and Pennsylvania, particularly at Jackson Va., Front Royal, Winchester, Cedar Mountain, Antietam, Fredericksburg, Chancellorsville and Gettysburg; went with his Reg. in 1863 to Tennessee and reenlisted in Jan. 1864; returned to his Reg. after a furlough of fifty days, and went with it in the great movement upon Atlanta; was in the battles of Resaca, Kenesaw, Peach Tree Creek and about Atlanta and after the capture of that City went under Gen. Sherman when he made his memorable march through Georgia and captured Savannah and through the Carolinas. After the surrender of Johnston's Army, Mr. Richardson returned to Washington with his Reg. and was discharged July 27. 1865 having served about four years and three months. This soldier has the honor of being one of the two men from Athol that were with Gen. Sherman in his Great March, and of being the only one of that invincible army that returned to Athol at the close of the war. He was made Corporal at the battle of Antietam and Sergeant April 1. 1864.

Neri F. Ripley, 21. Reg. (See page 125), went with his Reg. into service in North Carolina and was engaged at the capture of Roanoke Island but was sick at the time Newbern was captured. Being unfit for duty he was discharged Dec. 22.

1862, and died at Winchendon Jan. 16. 1863, of an abscess in the stomach brought on in the service. Mr. Ripley left a wife and two children in Winchendon but his remains were brought to Athol for interment.

Harvey Robbins, 27. Reg. (See page 128), was among the recruits that joined this Reg. in N. Carolina in 1862 in season to be in the battles at Kinston, Whitehall and Goldsboro' and also in the defence of Washington N. Carolina. His health was generally good but he was taken sick and died of a fever at Newbern June 29. 1863. Mr. Robbins left in Athol a wife and four children.

William J. Rogers, 36. Reg. (See page 131), joined his Reg. in the autumn of 1864 in front of Petersburg and was first in battle Sept. 30 when the 9th Corps to which the 36. Reg. belonged was repulsed with considerable loss. During the winter Mr. Rogers did garrison and picket duty in and about the Forts near Petersburg, particularly at Fort Rice and was on picket when the assault was made April 1. 1865 which was followed by the capture of Petersburg and Richmond and the surrender of Lee's Army. Mr. Rogers was discharged with his Reg. June 8. 1865 and returned home in health.

Emory Sawin, 36. Reg. (See page 131), joined the Reg. at Worcester and went with it to the seat of war in Virginia, and to Lexington Kentucky and later to recruit the army of Gen. Grant at Vicksburg; was in the fight at Jackson Miss. and other movements in that region till after Vicksburg fell; returned with his Reg. to Crab Orchard Kentucky where he was sick two months; was in the Hospital at Camp Nelson two months; three months in the Hospital at Portsmouth Grove R. I. and four months on duty there; was on duty nine months in Providence R. I. and two and one half months in Albany N. Y. and was discharged Aug. 11. 1865, the three years of his enlistment having expired.

Lewis H. Sawin, Navy, (See page 135), son of the above, entered the Navy in the Spring of 1862 and was attached during the whole period of his enlistment to the U. S. Ship Sonoma of 1000 tons that went from Portsmouth Navy Yard into service in James River Va. where Mr. Sawin remained till after the retirement of Gen. McClellan from the Peninsula in 1862. The Sonoma then went to the West Indies and after a cruise of nine months came North for repairs. After these were completed, Mr. Sawin sailed from New York to take part in the blockade of Charleston S. C. and the Sonoma remained in that service till the three years of his enlistment had expired. He was discharged March 6. 1885, having taken part in the capture of three prizes at the West Indies and one off Charleston.

Charles Sears, 27. Reg. (See page 128), joined his Reg. in North Carolina as a recruit in 1862 in season to be in the engagements at Kinston, Whitehall and Goldsboro'. Mr. Sears was also engaged during the defence of Washington N. C. and in the fight at Gum Swamp. While the Reg. was in Virginia he had charge of a plantation nine miles from Norfolk for a time and had the Small Pox there. Recovering he was in the engagement at Port Walthall and Arrowfield Church — and was carrying rations to the men when so many of his Reg. were captured at Drury's Bluff. Mr. Sears was afterwards in the battles at Coal Harbor and before Petersburg and was discharged with the expiration of his term of service Sept. 27. 1864.

Cutler Seaver, 42. Reg. (See page 140), enlisted for 100 days service without bounty and went with his Reg. to Great Falls Md. where he remained doing garrison duty till the term for which he had enlisted expired. He was discharged Nov. 15. 1864, but soon reentered the service and went into Camp at Readville where he was soon taken sick and died.

George R. Severance, 21. Reg. (See page 125), went with his Reg to Annapolis and into service in North Carolina, was in the engagements at Roanoke Island and at Newbern, but in what other battles or when or why he was discharged is unknown.

W. A. Shepardson, 21. Reg. (See page 125), went with his Reg. into service in North Carolina but no material facts in his history as a soldier from Athol have been ascertained.

Albert Simonds, 27. Reg. (See page 128), was among the recruits that joined this Reg. in North Carolina in the Autumn of 1862; was in the battles at Kinston, Whitehall and Goldsboro' and assisted in the defence of Washington N. C. and when the 27. Reg. was removed to Virginia in 1863 he was detailed to guard prisoners at Norfolk and continued to serve in this capacity till the time of his discharge Sept. 27. 1864 when he returned home in comfortable health.

Charles A. Simonds, 11. U. S. Inf. (See page 135), son of the above, went into the service in 1861 and was a Musician; was six months at Perryville Md. and had the Measles; recovering went with his Reg. to Alexandria and then into the Peninsular Campaign under Gen. McClellan;

was first in battle in six of the seven days conflict before Richmond and afterwards at Bull Run
No. 2. at Fredericksburg, Chancellorsville and at
Gettysburg where he was detailed for three
weeks' service in the Hospital as nurse; soon after which he was transferred to the Band and
sent to Fort Independence Boston Harbor where
he served till the three years of his enlistment
had expired.   He was discharged Oct. 3. 1864.

William O. Simonds, 11. U. S. Inf. (See page
135), brother of the above, went with him into
service in Maryland and Virginia, had the
Measles but recovered and was in the Peninsular
Campaign under Gen. McClellan and especially
was in six of the seven days battles before Richmond ; was in the 2d Bull Run fight and in the
engagements at Fredericksburg, Chancellorsville,
and Gettysburg and later in the Campaign under Gen. Grant as he moved towards Richmond ;
was taken prisoner in the battle of the Wilderness; was marched to Lynchburg and thence to
Danville and a little later to Andersonville ;
thence he was removed to Charleston where
with the imprisoned Union Officers he was exposed to the fire of our Navy for one week,
which was the best part of his imprisonment because he had enough to eat; then he was removed to the prison at Florence S. C. where he

remained four months with but little food and little clothing and with the Camp Fever to add to his sufferings ; was at length started for Salisbury N. C. but was taken to Richmond, paroled and sent to Annapolis for exchange and reached home in Feb. 1865 in comfortable health, having served three years and six months. At Gainsville a ball penetrated his blanket which was folded over his heart and passed through his coat and shirt and left a black spot upon his flesh; and at Gettysburg he was slightly wounded.

Henry N. Smith, 1. H. Artillery, (See page 134), went into service in 1863 but was in no engagement of considerable importance till May 1864. In the battle of Spottsylvania Mr. Smith was taken prisoner but the particulars of his sufferings and escape it has been impossible to learn. Nothing could be heard of him for many months but after great exposure he regained his liberty, rejoined his Regiment at Burkesville Va. and was mustered out of service with it.

Warren E. Smith, 53. Reg. (See page 123), went with his Reg. to Louisiana, and was in the engagement at the capture of Fort Bisland and in other service in that vicinity ; was sent sick to Brashear City from Vermillionville La.; rejoined his Company Aug. 9. and returned with it to Athol Aug. 24 1863, feeble but recovering.

Henry Smith, 27. Reg. (See page 128), was one of the recruits of 1862 that joined the Reg. in North Carolina, was Orderly for Col. Lee and served in this capacity in various expeditions but after the capture of his Colonel served for a time in the ranks. Mr. Smith reenlisted in Jan. 1864 but had his furlough later than his comrades and did not return to his Reg. He is supposed to have taken up his residence in Canada.

Joseph C. Smith, 27. Reg. (See page 128), went with his Reg. into service in North Carolina; was teamster and sick at the capture of Roanoke Island, but on duty at Newbern, Kinston, Whitehall and Goldsboro', also at the Siege of Washington, but his health failing he was discharged April 13. 1863.

Hubbard V. Smith, 2. Reg. (See page 123), was among the first to join the army from Athol at the breaking out of the Rebellion, and went with his Reg. into service on the Upper Potomac; was in the Shenandoah Campaign under Gen. Banks, and May 25. 1862 in the engagement near Strasburg Va. he was wounded, just as our troops were retreating. A Minie ball

entered his body just above the right hip and
passed so nearly through him that it was extracted above the left hip. An hour later he
was taken prisoner and kept two weeks at Winchester, when the rebels being obliged to retreat,
he was paroled for exchange. Seven weeks
later he was removed to the Hospital at Har-
per's Ferry and a week later, that place being
about to fall into the hands of the rebels, he was
sent to Annapolis. In Oct. 1862 he so far recovered as to be able to come home and was
discharged Jan. 1. 1863. Mr. Smith was but
partially recovered, and is still a great sufferer.

Henry H. Southland, 53. Reg. (See page 133),
went with his Reg. to Louisiana and Feb. 1. 1863
was detailed as Pioneer of Company E. Mr.
Southland was left sick at Baton Rouge April 1.
1863 and was not able to rejoin the Company
till Aug. 9. at which date he did so and returned
with his Reg. Aug. 24. 1863, in comfortable
health.

John W. Sprague, 12. Reg. (See page 124),
enlisted July 1. 1861 and was engaged for nearly
a year with his Reg. guarding the fords of the
Potomac. Later he was in the battles of Thor-
roughfare Gap, Bull Run No. 2. Chantilly, South
Mountain, Antietam, Fredericksburg, Chancel-

lorsville and Gettysburg; was sick with Chronic
Diarrhœa nearly a year, but was on duty nearly
all of the time; was struck on the left shoulder
at Bull Run by a ball that drew blood and pro-
duced a large contusion but was not very severely wounded; was taken prisoner the first
day of the contest at Gettysburg and was
marched from that place to Richmond 240 miles
in 22 days, with but little to eat beside the
grain plucked from the road side as the prisoners passed along; was confined in the rebel
prison at Belle Island nearly six months and
suffered there beyond description; was paroled
Dec. 28. 1863 but the men were so feeble that
it took from 9 o'clk in the morning till dark for
them to cross the city Richmond 2½ miles and
some of them made the journey upon their
hands and knees for more than half of the distance; reached Annapolis Dec. 29. and was
exchanged in May 1864. but remained after
recovering his strength to assist at the Hospital
till July 1. 1864 when he was discharged. Mr.
Sprague is now, Jan. 1866, a Police Officer on
duty in Boston.

Peter Stanton, **53.** Reg. (See page 133), went
with his Reg. to Louisiana and after being in the
engagement at Fort Bisland was sent from Opelousas to Brashear City May 5. 1863 wounded

in the finger by the accidental discharge of his
musket; rejoined his Comp. Aug. 11. and returned with it Aug. 24. 1863.   Later Mr. Stanton reentered the service in the 4th H. Artillery, but was discharged as unfit for service
before the Reg. left for the seat of war.

George W. Stevens, 3. Heavy Artillery (See
page 133), entered the service Jan. 1. 1863 and
was employed all of the time on garrison duty
in the various Forts near Washington till the
close of the war.   Mr. Stevens was mustered
out of the service Sept. 18. 1865 and returned
to Athol in health.

Harrison Stockwell, 53. Reg. (See page 133),
went with the Reg. to Louisiana but was left
sick at Camp Kearney Carrollton March 6. 1863.
Mr. Stockwell rejoined his Company when the
sick were collected Aug. 11. and returned with
it Aug. 24. 1863.

Spencer Stockwell, 53. Reg. (See page 133),
went with his Company into Camp at Groton
Junction, but was soon taken sick with the
Diphtheria and died there Nov. 20. 1862.   His
remains were brought to Athol for burial, and
his funeral was attended by a very large concourse of people in the Church of the Evangeli-

cal Society, Nov. 23. 1862. This was the first death in Company E, 53. Reg.

Henry H. Stratton, 53. Reg. (See page 133), went into service in Louisiana and after being with his Reg. in all its previous engagements and marches up to June 14. 1863. was wounded in the head in the assault of that day upon Port Hudson, and was sent to St Louis Hospital at New Orleans. Recovering, he rejoined his Company Aug. 7. and returned with it in health to Athol Aug. 24. 1863.

Frederic A. Stratton, 53. Reg. and 56. (See page 133), was in the Regular Army for seven months in 1860; was made Corporal in Co. E 53. Reg. Oct. 17. 1862 and was with his Reg. at Fort Bisland, and in all its marches and engagements till after the fall of Port Hudson when he was sent sick to Baton Rouge. Mr. Stratton came with the sick in the St. Mary's to New York and reached home Aug. 20. 1864. He reentered the service in the 56. Reg. in Feb. 1865, and was engaged in the battles which ended in the capture of Petersburg in April. May 1. 1865 he was detailed Orderly for Medical Director Dr. Adams and served till discharged with his Reg. July 22. 1865.

Florence Sullivan, 1. H. Artillery (See page 134), was with his Reg. in 1864. in the battles at Spottsylvania Court House, No. Anna, Tolopotomy, Coal Harbor, before Petersburg in June 1864., at Strawberry Plains and Deep Bottom, in the last of which Aug. 16. 1864 he was severely wounded by a ball that passed through his left thigh and into the leg of a comrade behind him. Recovering, he took part in the Weldon R. Road Raid at Hatcher's Run and in the capture of Petersburg. He was discharged with his Reg.

Charles E. Taft, 21. Reg. (See page 125), joined the Reg. early in 1864 and went into service in Virginia; was sick one month at Washington; was first under fire at the explosion of the Mine in front of Petersburg July 30.; was in the Weldon Rail Road engagement and in the fight at Pegram Farm and when the Rebels charged upon and took Fort Steadman; was in the great battles near Petersburg in April 1865 and a few days later when the rebel army was defeated below Richmond and surrendered. Mr. Taft was mustered out of the U. S. Service July 13. 1865.

Clinton Teel, 4. H. Artillery (See page 135), enlisted for and served one year; was engaged during the whole period of his service doing garrison duty in the various Forts in and about Washington and was discharged, in health, July 17. 1865.

George L. Tenney, 5. Reg. (See page 123), enlisted for, and served 100 days and was employed during the period of his service in doing garrison duty in and near Baltimore.

Horace O. Thayer, 56. Reg. (See page 134), went into camp with this Reg. at Readville in the autumn of 1863 but before it went to the seat of war was taken sick of Brain Fever and died at Readville Feb. 2. 1864, after a sickness of five days. His remains were brought to Athol for interment and buried from the Methodist Episcopal Church Feb. 7. 1864.

Lauriston A. Thorpe, 27. Reg. (See page 128), went with his Reg. into service in North Carolina and after being engaged in the battles at Roanoke Island, Newbern and other places was sent to the Hospital sick. Recovering, Mr. Thorpe was detailed as nurse in the Foster Gen. Hospital at Newbern where he served one year or more when he was transferred to the Dispensary of the same Hospital. In this he served about one year when the period of his enlistment expired. The Yellow Fever was prevailing at Newbern and the ship upon which Mr. Thorpe embarked for home was sent into Quarantine at Fortress Monroe, and there he died of this disease Oct. 7. 1864, while his friends were looking most anxiously for his return. Funeral services were attended in the Methodist Episcopal Church Oct. 23. 1864.

William L. Thrower, 53. Reg. (See page 133), went with his Reg. to Louisiana but was left sick at Baton Rouge April 1. 1863; recovered to rejoin his Company July 14. and returned with it in comfortable health Aug. 24. 1863.

Robert W. Thrower, 27. Reg. (See page 128), went with his Reg. to North Carolina; was in the battle at Roanoke Island, but was sick and on board a transport at the battle of Newbern, was landed at Newbern and died there of a Lung Fever March 31. 1862. Mr. Thrower was buried at Newbern.

Charles Tilden, 30. Reg. (See page 129), enlisted Nov. 7. 1861, but was discharged at Camp Chase Lowell Dec. 15. of the same year. Cause, Disability.

Edward L. Townsend, 2. Reg. (See page 123), was among the first to enlist from Athol and went with his Reg. to the Upper Potomac ; was engaged during Gen. Banks's advance and retreat in the Shenandoah Valley and in the battle at Antietam ; soon after which he was transferred at his own request to the 4th U. S. Artillery in which he served till the time of his enlistment expired. Up to Jan. 1864 he had been wounded five times.

George D. Townsend, 27. Reg. (See page 128), went with his Reg. to N. Carolina ; was in the battles at Roanoke Island, Kinston, Whitehall and Goldsboro', assisted in the defence of Washington N. C.; Reenlisted Jan. 1864, and was sick till Jan. 1865. ; returned to his Reg. to be taken prisoner in the conflict near Kinston N. C. March 8.; was paroled for exchange and discharged at Annapolis June 15. 1865.

Henry T. Townsend, 32. Reg. (See page 130), enlisted in Feb. 1862 in what was then the 1st Battalion at Fort Warren, but his health failing he was discharged June 21. of the same year, soon after his Reg. had left for the seat of war.

Harlan P. Townsend, 53. Reg. (See page 133), was detailed as Assistant Cook of Company E Oct. 1862 and went with the Reg. to Louisiana; returned to the ranks March 1. 1863 and was with the Reg. participating in all its marches and the captures of Fort Bisland and Port Hudson and came home in health with his Company Aug. 24. 1863.

William I. Turner, 5. Reg. (See page 123), enlisted for and served 100 days; and during the period of his enlistment was employed doing garrison duty in the Forts in and near Baltimore.

Nathaniel B. Twichell, 27. Reg. (See page 128), joined his Reg. in North Carolina as one of the recruits of 1862; was in the engagements at Kinston, Whitehall, Goldsboro', the siege of Washington N. C. and at Gum Swamp; was made Corporal Feb. 20. 1863; reenlisted Jan. 1864 and had a furlough; returned to his Reg. to be in the engagement at Port Walthall Va. and at Arrowfield Church, was killed in the last mentioned by a ball that struck his head, dying instantly and leaving in Athol a wife and two children. Mrs. Twichell lost one brother in the Hospital at N. Orleans and another a prisoner at Andersonville. Mr. Twichell was killed May 9. 1864.

Willard Twichell, 11. U. S. Inf. (See page 135), joined this Reg. early in the war; was cook but was in all the battles with his musket; was in six of the seven days conflicts before Richmond in 1862, also at Fredericksburg, Chancellorsville and Gettysburg, was in the battles of the Wilderness, Spottsylvania, No. Anna and was killed in the engagement June 24. 1864 before Petersburg. A ball passed through his abdomen June 24. and he died June 27.

Charles H. Tyler, 53. Reg. (See page 133), went with his Reg. to Louisiana and was in the fight at the capture of Fort Bisland; marched with the Reg. to Opelousas but was sent from that place sick to Brashear City May 5. 1863: was taken prisoner at Brashear City June 23.; went to Ship Island July 9.; returned to N. Orleans and rejoined his Reg. Aug. 11. and came home with it, feeble but recovering, Aug. 24. 1863.

Freeman H. Walker, 53. Reg. (See page 133), went with his Reg. into service in Louisiana; was in the battle at Fort Bisland and in the marches to Alexandria and to Port Hudson; was sent from before Port Hudson June 6. to Baton Rouge sick; embarked on board the St. Mary's for N. York and arrived Aug. 14. Mr. Walker reached Athol. Aug. 20. 1863, feeble but recovering.

22*

David Walker, 53. Reg. (See page 133), went to Louisiana and was with the Reg. in all its battles and marches from the movement upon the enemy near Fort Bisland to the capture of Port Hudson and returned in health Aug. 24. 1863.

Ransom Ward, 79. U. S. (Col.) Inf. (See page 137), was engaged in the winter of 1862 in the secret service of the Government in Kansas and in the summer of the same year was commissioned Captain of Co. H. 1. Kansas Colored Infantry, now designated the 79 U. S. Infantry. This was the first colored Reg. armed and put into the field with the U. S. forces, and no Reg. at the West has ranked higher for efficiency and discipline. Capt. Ward led his men honorably in the following engagements; Island Mound, Sherwood Mission, Cabin Creek, Honey Springs, Poison Springs, Flat Rock near Fort Gibson and at the capture of Fort Smith. Most of these engagements were in the Indian Territory. Capt. Ward was discharged Nov. 9. 1865, worn out with his hard service but gaining. His Brother, Lieut. Col. Gardner Ward, formerly of Athol, commanded the 79. U. S. Reg.

Jonathan D. Ward, 21. Reg. (See page 125), went with his Reg. to N. Carolina and was in the engagements at Roanoke Island and Newbern, when he was taken sick with a Fever which rendered him unfit for duty and he was discharged Jan. 22. 1863. Mr. Ward probably counted upon the quota of Orange but his home for a number of years has been in Athol.

William Washburn, 36. Reg. (See page 131), was with his Reg. in Maryland, Virginia, Kentucky, Ohio and at the siege of Vicksburg. After the surrender of Vicksburg he returned with his Reg. to Kentucky; and was sick with the Dumb Ague, at Camp Park near Nicholasville Ky. where he died after a sickness of 10 days. The date of his death is Sept. 5. 1863. He left in Athol a wife and five children.

Oscar Washburn, 27. Reg. (See page 128), son of the above, joined the Reg. at Norfolk after the close of its first North Carolina Campaigns; went with it to Suffolk and Yorktown, was sick three months, falling out on the march to Coal Harbor; was detailed Orderly for Surgeon Williams and discharged July 17. 1865.

Theodore Washburn, 27. Reg. (See page 128), went with his Reg. for the Town of Phillipston, into service in N. Carolina having had the Measles at Annapolis; was engaged at Roanoke Island and Newbern, also in the defence of Washington N. C. and at Gum Swamp; reenlisted for Athol; was kept on duty at Norfolk while the Campaign of 1864 was in progress in Va. was taken prisoner near Kinston March 8. 1865, but was soon paroled at Richmond and sent to Annapolis, where he was discharged in health June 15. 1866.

Horace K. Weaver, 32. Reg. (See page 130), went with his Reg. from Fort Warren to Washington and Harrison's Landing Va. was in the battles at Antietam, Fredericksburg, Chancellorsville and Gettysburg; moved under Gen. Grant in May 1864; was in the battle of the Wilderness and was sunstruck during the engagement at Spottsylvania. Recovering Mr. Weaver was in various other engagements of less importance till the three years of his enlistment had expired, and he was mustered out of the service Nov. 26. 1864.

Maxon R. Wetherby, 15. Reg. (See page 124), was drafted in 1863, held to serve and reported for duty; joined his Reg. Aug. 15. in Virginia and was with it in various services in that State till he was discharged.

Edmund R. West, 24. Reg. (See page 126). This soldier is known to have gone into service in the 24. Reg. from Athol, and to have served at Roanoke Island and in other engagements in N. Carolina ; to have gone with his Reg. to Morris' Island and to have been engaged there and to have gone to St. Augustine Florida where he was taken prisoner, Dec. 30. 1863, since which date nothing has been heard of him by those in charge of this Record, tho' diligent inquiry has been made.   E. West, Comp. A. 24th Reg. died a prisoner at Andersonville Ga., May 24. 1864, and the No. of his grave is 1334.   There is reason to suppose this refers to E. R. West, whose history is here given.

E. Whipple Whitney, 27. Reg. (See page 128), was one of the company of recruits that joined this Reg. in N. Carolina in the autumn of 1862 and went on the Expedition to Kinston, Whitehall and Goldsboro'.   Mr. Whitney had been but a little time in service before he was unfitted for duty by an injury to one of his eyes and later by the permanent disabling of one of his fingers and he was discharged Aug. 15. 1863.   After his return home he was unable to labor for many months.

Chandler Whitney, 30. Reg. (See page 129), went into camp with this Reg. in Pittsfield but died Feb. 1. 1862 after an illness of three weeks.

His remains were brought to Athol for interment and he left a wife in this town.

Alfred G. Williams, 11. Reg. (See page 123), was appointed Assistant Surgeon of this Reg. and joined it in Virginia; was on duty during the battles at Williamsburg, Hanover Court House, the 2d engagement at Fair Oaks, at Savage's Station, Willis Church and then at Malvern Hill, but his health failing, he resigned and was discharged Aug. 18. 1862 with the most honorable testimonials. Jan. 27. 1863 he reentered the service as a Contract Surgeon and was assigned to the Hospital Boat, Nashville, on the Mississippi River, where he remained till ill health again compelled him to request his discharge. This part of his service lasted four months. His last service was rendered at Elmira New York as a Surgeon in the Hospital of rebel prisoners and this continued for the period of six months, when Dr. Williams returned to Athol, but has more recently removed to No. Adams.

Nelson G. Wood, 27. Reg. (See page 128), joined his Reg. as one of the recruits of 1862 and was with it in the engagements at Kinston, Whitehall, Goldsboro', as well as in the defence of Washington N. C. and at Gum Swamp; went with his Reg. into service in Virginia; was in the engagements at Port Walthall and Arrowfield Church and was killed in the latter, May 9. 1864. Mr. Wood with others of his Company was lying on the ground when he was struck by a shot and died instantly. He was buried near by.

George B. Wood, 53. Reg. (See page 133), went with his Reg. into camp at Groton Junction and with it to New York; was sick there and removed to Shutesbury his native town where he died Jan. 2. 1863 having been discharged from the service the day before. He was buried at Shutesbury.

Thomas A. Woodward, 30. Reg. (See page 129), went with his Reg. under Gen. Butler to Louisiana and was with it in the capture of New Orleans and in much other service in that Department including the Capture of Port Hudson. Mr. Woodward reenlisted in 1864 and was with his Reg. in the Campaigns in Virginia which resulted in the fall of Richmond. He is at this time (Jan. 1866.) still in service in the vicinity of Richmond.

Asa Wyman, 36. Reg. (See page 131), went with his Reg. into service in Va. and with it to Kentucky, Ohio and Mississippi; was in the engagement at Jackson and in service back of

Vicksburg till after its surrender; was sent in the sick boat up the Mississippi and removed to Annapolis where he died of a Fever and Chronic Diarrhœa May 3. 1864. Mr. Wyman was for a considerable period cook for his Company.

Morgan Young, 21. Reg. (See page 125), was an old soldier having been for five years in the Regular Army and engaged in the war in Florida; went with the 21. Reg. to N. Carolina and was in the engagements at Roanoke Island, Newbern and Camden; was in the 2d Bull Run battle and afterward in service in Kentucky and Tennessee; was sick a part of the time; offered to reenlist but did not pass the requisite examination and finally served out the three years of his enlistment as Cook in some Hospital.

www.ingramcontent.com/pod-product-compliance
Lightning Source LLC
Chambersburg PA
CBHW030641030726
47497CB00006B/1888